CHILDREN'S LIVELY MINDS

Other Redleaf Press Books by Deb Curtis with Margie Carter

The Art of Awareness, Second Edition
Designs for Living and Learning, Second Edition
Learning Together with Young Children, Second Edition
Reflecting Children's Lives, Second Edition
Reflecting in Communities of Practice
The Visionary Director, Second Edition

Children's Lively Minds

SCHEMA THEORY
MADE VISIBLE

by Deb Curtis and Nadia Jaboneta

Redleaf Press®
www.redleafpress.org
800-423-8309

Published by Redleaf Press
10 Yorkton Court
St. Paul, MN 55117
www.redleafpress.org

First edition 2019
Senior editor: Heidi Hogg
Managing editor: Douglas Schmitz
Cover design: Erin Kirk New
Cover photographs: Deb Curtis and Nadia Jaboneta
Interior design: Erin Kirk New
Typeset in Garamond Premier Pro and Brother 1816
Interior photographs: Deb Curtis, Nadia Jaboneta, Matthew Steven
    Lawrence, Riley Graham, Darby Hillyard, and Mahroushka Papazian

Printed in the United States of America

Library of Congress Cataloging-in-Publication Data
Names: Curtis, Deb, author. | Jaboneta, Nadia, author.
Title: Children's lively minds : schema theory made visible / by Deb Curtis
    and Nadia Jaboneta.
Description: St. Paul, MN : Redleaf Press, [2019] | Includes bibliographical
    references.
Identifiers: LCCN 2018054959 (print) | LCCN 2019006236 (ebook) | ISBN
    9781605546957 (e-book) | ISBN 9781605546940 (pbk : alk. paper)
Subjects: LCSH: Child psychology. | Repetition compulsion. | Human behavior.
    | Educational psychology. | Reflective teaching.
Classification: LCC BF721 (ebook) | LCC BF721 .C87 2019 (print) | DDC
    155.4—dc23
LC record available at https://urldefense.proofpoint.com/v2/url?u=https-3A
    __lccn.loc.gov_2018054959&d=DwIFAg&c=euGZstcaTDllvimEN8b7j
    XrwqOf-v5A_CdpgnVfiiMM&r=gX7U_27BtUCeFTyI7PMJ4yl8ifrCjuxqZQ
    NBnwQelXg&m=P5Wjd3H3Xt-GFKCMDamuIBSxS4N4XGyBAGHCftg2G
    tA&s=c7azCFTnlqKznIq3PjpnxEvkGjzDT97FHMnMversly0&e=

Printed on acid-free paper   U21-11

To my mom and dad, who always encouraged me to dig deep, think, and learn. Hope wherever they are, they can see how far I've come. —Deb

To my family, who loved and supported me throughout this journey. Gracias familia! —Love, Nadia

Contents

Acknowledgments

I'm grateful to the children, families, and teachers at Epiphany Early Learning Preschool in Seattle, Washington, where most of my delightful stories for this book were collected. I send great appreciation to the educators in the Reflective Teacher Cohorts, who paused, marveled, and studied children with me, from Southwest Human Development, Phoenix, Arizona; First Five, San Francisco, California; Sound Child Care Solutions, Seattle, Washington; Manitoba Child Care Association, Winnipeg, Canada; Our Neighborhood Child Development Center, Charlottesville, Virginia; Highland Presbyterian Preschool, Louisville, Kentucky; and Second Presbyterian Weekday School, Louisville, Kentucky. To our colleagues in Aotearoa–New Zealand, in particular the educators from Tots Corner and Magic Garden Care and Education Centers, who first introduced us to schema theory. Thanks for many of the beautiful photos shared by the Highlander School, Atlanta, Georgia; Compass Child Development centers in Peterborough, Ontario, Canada; and St. Mark Lutheran Preschool, Charlottesville, VA. And special thanks to Nadia Jaboneta and Brian Silveira, who join me in the early childhood nerds club, noticing, savoring, and sharing the tiniest details of children's amazing ways. We learn so much together!
—Deb

I would like to start by thanking my mentors Sarah Johnson, Mia Cavalca, Daniel Meier, and Barbara Henderson from San Francisco State University, who all helped guide me in the beginning of my work in the early childhood field. A big thanks to the educators in New Zealand for sharing their knowledge of schema theory and inspiring me with their passion for working with young children. Thank you to Margie Carter for leading this INSPIRE study tour. It was a transformative experience, and I am grateful for her guidance. My deepest thanks to my directors Belann Giarretto and Lynn Turner, who have been extremely encouraging along my journey. I could not do the work that I do without their support and leadership! I am grateful for my thinking partner and friend Brian Silveira. We have learned so much in our reflective work together these past ten years. I would like to express my gratitude to my friend Deb Curtis for inviting me to collaborate on this book and continuously inspiring me. It has been a joy to pause and marvel together! Thank you to our editors and designers at Redleaf Press for helping make our idea for this book come to life. A big thank-you to all the children who have been "Coyotes" in my classroom—you have all motivated me and taught me how to see the endless possibilities in play. A thank-you to all the children's families for letting us share these amazing stories and photos. I'm appreciative of my teaching team, Darby Hillyard and Riley Graham. They were always eager to join me in studying the children's work and learning together. Finally, I would like to thank my family for their endless love and support and for believing in me: my husband, Jim; my daughters, Ari and Leelah; my parents, Nelly and Enrique, and my sister, Violeta. I could not have written this book without them.

—Nadia

CHAPTER 1

Lively Minds at Work

We want to know what the children think, feel, and wonder. We believe that the children will have things to tell each other and us that we have never heard before. We are always listening for a surprise and the birth of a new idea. This practice supports a . . . searching together for new meaning. Together, we become a community of seekers. —Louise Cadwell

The children eagerly approached the table, which displayed an arrangement of brand-new boxes of chalk pastels and paper. As we expected, several children began to draw pictures. One child had a different idea. He drew alternating lines of different colors across the paper. After working this way for a while, he used his hands to rub and smear the chalk lines. Other children noticed his discovery and began to spread the chalk across their papers too.

Teacher Nadia offered tissues for rubbing the chalk pastels, and changing the chalk drawings with the tissue became the work of the entire group.

The children noticed that when they applied pressure while drawing with the pastels, powder formed. Creating powder became the new quest, and several children invested in making piles of chalk dust. Rubbing, moving, mounding, scattering, and blowing the dust were the many ways the children investigated this shimmering substance. Next, one child decided to wet the tissue to see how water would change the chalk.

Mixing water and chalk inspired further discoveries. The children requested more water, and small cups of water served as vessels for mixing chalk dust to change the color of the water. Eager to see more transformations, the children found sticks to use as tools for making

more dust. They quickly learned to shave the chalk into smaller pieces, and then to mix it into the water, creating a thick liquid. The children worked fervently on these many investigations for over an hour.

But pastels are for drawing!

As the children's work unfolded, Deb and Nadia questioned one another at several junctions—should we support and extend what they were doing with the pastels or redirect them? Our adult response was to protect the expensive pastels, which we offered as an art tool for careful drawing. We asked ourselves, "Is this a waste or destruction of materials? Will it get too messy? Should we help children use the pastels in the correct way? What value do we see in their work?" To become reflective teachers, we must momentarily suspend our adult views to pause, notice, and understand that rich, cooperative learning occurs when children pursue and share ideas and questions. We want to always be listening for the "birth of a new idea," as Louise Cadwell so eloquently reminds us. With a closer look, we determined that the children were remarkable in their use of observation, problem solving, and cause and effect to delve deeply into learning together with the materials. They used their own thinking and collaborated around one another's ideas and actions. They shared an all-consuming interest in transforming the chalk and invented tools and unique strategies to accomplish this goal. We decided to help this play grow because we saw that, rather than an art activity, this experience sparked the children's natural drive to take action to learn about the world.

Children Are Learning Machines

Children see more, hear more, feel more and experience more than adults do. They are far better learners than we are. These remarkable learning abilities reflect special features of children's brains, features that may actually make young children more conscious than adults. —Alison Gopnik

In her research on brain development and learning, Alison Gopnik describes young children as "learning machines." She explains that researchers have found that children are better learners than the most advanced computers or brilliant scientists. Children are voracious investigators, tinkering with and studying everything around them. They are naturally propelled to take action to test hypotheses and

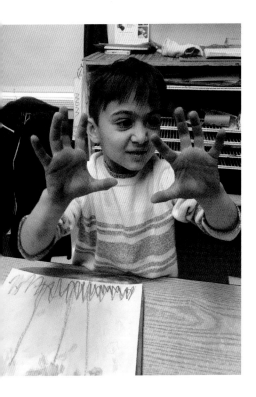

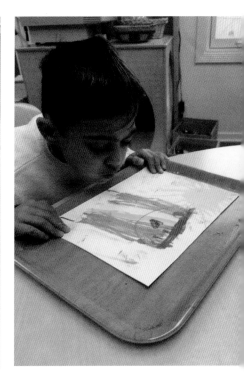

study the world in a systematic way. During explorations, children develop expectations and understandings and constantly test new ideas. They experiment and use trial and error, making discoveries about themselves and the magical world around them (Gopnik 2009).

Together we—Deb and Nadia—have a combined fifty-plus years of experiences working with young children, Deb as a preschool and toddler teacher in Seattle, Washington, and Nadia as a preschool teacher in San Francisco, California. Over the last several years, we have been cultivating our work as reflective teachers. We observe the details of children's competence closely and think together about the possible meaning and responses we might offer. We are studying Gopnik's research and the research of others on young children's brain development and learning, and we actively work to connect said research to our day-to-day practices in the classroom. Our story of transforming chalk is one of many we have collected that illustrates the findings we have learned from our studies. Seeing children's competence in these moments transforms our ideas about the education of young children and the role we play to enhance their amazing capacities for learning. We resist the current early education narrative that suggests children need to be readied for academic performance and the job market. We avoid quick fixes and strategies for curriculum planning and behavior management. We don't ask ourselves anymore what is working or not working to help children learn. Instead, we ask what is happening that reflects the details of children's deep desire and skills for learning. The outcomes we strive for are the ones we saw as the children worked together with the pastels. We value the creativity, inventiveness, and collaboration this experience offered them, much more than we value children sitting still and listening to a teacher to learn. Rather than documenting limited outcomes on checklists to get children ready for the future, we see our role as an unfolding process, where we recognize, study, and follow the children's lead, to support and enhance the remarkable capacities they already possess for living and learning fully together now.

We were thrilled to see brain research made visible as we observed the children's work with the pastels. We definitely saw their skillful and varied methods for investigating the materials. They were "learning machines" at work, using close observation, trying out many ideas, consciously repeating actions, making discoveries, and applying new understandings to go deeper into their work. And they did all this together seamlessly.

Super Sensory Beings

All of us collect fortunes when we are children—a fortune of colors, of light and darkness, of movements, of tensions. Some of us have the fantastic chance to go back to our fortune when we grow up. Most of us don't have that chance—that is the tragedy. —Ingmar Bergman

Research suggests that children have very flexible brains. Scientists describe this as "brain plasticity." The nature of children's brain structure allows them to actually see more, hear more, and experience feelings more intensely than adults. They take in large amounts of sensory information, and as they investigate and act on sensory input, they form brain pathways for all their future learning and capabilities.

Early experiences provide the main foundations in the brain for all the other connections to grow. This can be likened to the main freeways in a city. These larger freeways are where smaller streets and roads connect and the grid expands. The smaller complex connections and pathways cannot exist without the main, larger pathways to grow from. The more experiences children engage with, the more pathways they will form in their brains.

The overarching idea emerging from our study of brain development is that children are super sensory beings with astonishing inborn capacities for learning. It is our work to look closely for children's competencies and to understand the deeper significance of children's play, to take action and support them so they grow to their fullest potential.

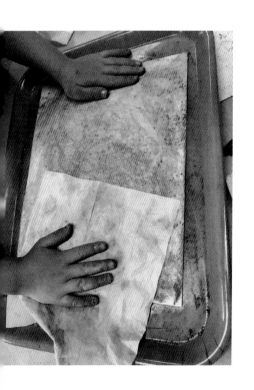

As early childhood educators, we know the importance of sensory, motor, and problem-solving experiences but often reduce our thinking about these vital aspects of children's development to prescribed curriculum activities, sensory tables, and finger paint. As we come to more deeply understand the magnitude of these experiences on children's brain development, we must take a closer look at what we provide. What do the environment and materials actually offer children for their brain development? What can they see, hear, touch, smell, or taste? How can we provide interesting possibilities and problems for them to take up? What is available to challenge their bodies as well as their minds?

When reflecting on the chalk story above, think about the strong sensory appeal of this experience. The children were fascinated with the power they had to transform the pastels, from smooth lines to powdery piles to goopy liquid. Their actions magically changed the colors of the chalk, from light pastels to vibrant, thick colors. During this multifaceted exploration, we understand they were building vital, lasting brain connections about how the world works and the power of their ideas and initiative to make an impact. We strive to use the deeper understandings we gain from reflecting on these moments to provide more meaningful materials and experiences that will grow children's remarkable abilities.

Schema Theory

Often over the years we've spent teaching, many of the sensory explorations, experimentations, and theory testing we've seen young children engage with, like the destruction of the chalk at the beginning of this chapter, have driven us a little crazy. Perhaps you have felt the same when watching children engage in the following behaviors:

- mixing together all the paints that you carefully organized by color
- dumping every toy and material from baskets into a giant pile
- moving toys and materials from place to place with seemingly no plan for how to use them
- crashing an elaborate block structure to the ground
- zooming and throwing cars and balls all over the classroom
- swiping all the toys off a tabletop or shelf
- standing on and jumping off everything
- hiding under a table or getting in any box or container
- tilting back on chairs, almost falling over

It seems no matter what we do or say to stop these sorts of behaviors, the children keep doing them. In the past, we learned to live with these behaviors, often acting as the preschool police to keep the frustrating undertakings to a minimum. But since learning about schema theory from our colleagues in New Zealand, we are no longer the same teachers we once were. Our point of view about these challenging behaviors, and our teaching practices in response to them, have been forever changed.

In our effort to learn more about schema theory, we returned to the work of psychologist and theorist Jean Piaget. He described a *schema* as a thread of thought that is demonstrated by repeated patterns in children's play, meaning that children's play is a reflection of deeper internally and specifically directed thoughts. When children are exploring schemas, they are building understandings of abstract ideas, patterns, and concepts.

Although Piaget has extensive research and theories about children's cognitive development, we have been most interested in his work about schemas as studied and described by Chris Athey, Cathy Nutbrown, and others from the United Kingdom and New Zealand. Their research, found in the various books, articles, and blogs they have written about repeated patterns in children's play, has become a valuable resource for our learning related to children's actions in play and their significance. Here are the schemas we have taken up in our own informal teacher research, along with some examples of how the children in your care may explore them:

- *Transporting*: Picking things up, moving them, and putting them down or dumping them.

- *Transforming*: Using materials to explore changes in shape, color, consistency, and so on.

- *Trajectory*: Exploring the horizontal, vertical, and diagonal movement of things and self. Making things fly through the air and moving self.

- *Rotation* and *Circularity*: Experimenting with things that turn—self, wheels, balls; exploring curved lines and circles.

- *Enclosing* and *Enveloping*: Surrounding objects with other things. Using self to get inside a defined area like blocks or boxes. Hiding, covering, or wrapping self and other things completely.

- *Connecting* and *Disconnecting*: Joining things together and tying things up. Taking things apart. Scattering things by using arms or legs. Wiping all toys or objects off a surface.
- *Positioning* and *Ordering*: Lining up toy cars; standing toy animals in line next to one another; sorting, classifying, and placing objects in proper order.
- *Orientation* and *Perspective*: Climbing everything, sitting upside down, hanging from bars, looking through holes and transparent objects, standing on toys, crawling under tables.

What about the Chalk?

Exploring the *transformation* schema was central to the work the children did to investigate the pastels in the story above. From our point of view, the quest to transform the chalk was compelling the children's attention and spurred the inventions of tools and actions to change the chalk in as many ways as possible. This story, like many others in this book, clearly demonstrates how children are born with brains that are active and wide open to the rich, sensory world around them. They are keen observers, able to see the smallest possibilities, from the dust they created with the chalk to the blazing color changes they created with the chalk dust and water. Then, as they take in this abundance of information, they have a remarkable, intuitive intelligence to repeat actions over and over again through schema explorations, to work together, to make discoveries, and to build lasting brain connections. As we have come to know and appreciate these inborn abilities, our patience, excitement, and commitment to do our best work on behalf of the children grows.

Not a Book to Fix Problems

To enter into a style of teaching which is based on questioning what we're doing and why, on listening to children, on thinking about how theory is translated into practice and how practice informs theory, is to enter into a way of working where professional development takes place day after day in the classroom. —Sonya Shoptaugh

This book is not about finding quick fixes or right answers. It is also not about the next curriculum activity or new trend to keep children busy. This book is focused on reflective practice in the spirit of the Sonya Shoptaugh quote above. It is a collection of stories of children's play that have inspired us to pause and marvel about the amazing children we get to spend our days with. Along with each story, we

offer brief references to the ideas, theories, and research we draw on for more insight. Our work may spark your interest in doing your own research. There is an abundance of findings to consider when thinking about work with children, and there isn't one correct answer, nor will we attempt to offer you any definitive information here. Instead, we will search for many possibilities for understanding what we see unfolding with the children so we can make choices about the role we want to play in enhancing experiences for all of us. Seeking deeper meaning in what we observe heightens our joy of the day-to-day work and gives us insight into the power we have to shape a brighter future.

We both regularly serve as mentor teachers, thinking together with other teachers about work with children. We are not scientists or professional researchers. We see ourselves as informal teacher-researchers and early childhood nerds, always alert to new information, and we immediately try to find real-life examples of what we read and hear in our daily work with children. We continually challenge each other to find connections between the research, theory, and our practice. We love to construct our own understandings and expand on the ideas we learn about. We regularly text back and forth, sharing stories of children that reflect the new ideas we are pursuing together. We see ourselves as social justice educators, seeking multiple perspectives and equity in our daily work with children. This includes being fierce advocates for childhood and children's rights, particularly for active play. Our shared journey has been a source of intellectual, social, and even spiritual development as teachers and friends.

How to Use This Book

We wrote this book because we are eager to deepen our own thinking, learning, and teaching practices. We also find that whenever we share information about brain development and schema theory and how they relate to our work with children, teachers are always eager to hear more and offer their own stories. If more early educators share stories of children's competence for learning together, we believe it will transform how children are seen by teachers, administrators, and policy makers. We can think of no more important work for the future of our children, ourselves, educational systems, and the world.

Chapter 2: Identifying Schemas—Seeing Underneath Children's Ordinary, Challenging Behaviors is divided into stories and photos that reflect each of the specific schemas we have chosen to highlight. Following each story, we offer our reflections and questions and include ideas about the significance we see and the possibilities for further learning and study.

In chapter 3: Schema Explorations—A Strong Force in Children's Learning and Development, we use stories to describe how we see schema explorations drive children's learning in many domains, including fostering identity, social connections, and collaboration; promoting math skills; and enhancing play scripts for imaginative play. We also explore the vital connection between schema explorations and active play for brain development.

Chapter 4: Environments and Materials to Invite Schema Explorations offers photos and descriptions of environments and collections of materials, and the rationale behind why we believe they provoke deep engagement in children.

Chapter 5: Making Schema Explorations and Learning Visible shows the power of sharing information about schema theory with children, families, and colleagues.

We hope the detailed descriptions of play that we offer in this book will delight you and grow your respect for children's competence. Perhaps you will be encouraged to pause, marvel, and study the significance you find in your own work with children.

Dip in and out of our stories to jump-start your thinking about what you see children doing. Then go find your own stories, intriguing theories, and research and join us in the pleasure, satisfaction, and powerful impact that reflective practice brings to your work and, in turn, the world.

CHAPTER 2

Identifying Schemas—Seeing Underneath Children's Ordinary, Challenging Behaviors

In psychology and cognitive science, *schema* is described as a pattern of thought or behavior, a system of organizing, or a mental structure for perceiving new information. Individuals use schemas to organize knowledge and to categorize objects and events based on common elements and characteristics. They do this to interpret and make predictions about the world.

In Jean Piaget's theory of development, children construct a series of schemas, or cognitive structures, that develop from repeated patterns and actions in their play. Schema explorations link together in clusters, which enable the development of more complex forms of learning (Piaget 1952).

These patterns of play first identified by Piaget were made more visible through research done by Chris Athey (2007). Schema play has been comprehensively studied in the United Kingdom and New Zealand to show how recognizing and providing for schema explorations supports learning and development in young children.

Advances in brain research, with the development of MRI and CAT scans, help us know much more about the process of learning as it happens in the brain. Neuroscientists can actually see brain cells communicate with one another and develop connections. These new findings about how permanent brain pathways are created have important implications in understanding schema explorations in young children. When children engage in repetitive play activities— a natural tendency—they grow and reinforce neural pathways in their brains, helping those pathways become permanent, which aids children when they consolidate learning and develop new understandings. Current research offers further confirmation of the vital role of play in young children's lives (Atherton and Nutbrown 2016).

Although there are complex theories explaining schema play, schemas are very easy to identify because they are actions that children engage in every day, all day long, over and over again. Adults often overlook or hamper schema investigations because they seem so simple and can be messy, destructive, and annoying. Making yourself aware of these typical patterns of behavior will enable you to appreciate children's deep, natural interests and extraordinary abilities. When you closely observe schema play, you can plan for and extend experiences where children engage in this essential work to build their brains.

This chapter is organized to help you identify schemas in children's play. More than forty schema behaviors have been identified by researchers, but in this book, we focus on those we see most often:

- *Transporting*
- *Transforming*
- *Trajectory*
- *Rotation* and *Circularity*
- *Enclosing* and *Enveloping*
- *Connecting* and *Disconnecting*
- *Positioning* and *Ordering*
- *Orientation* and *Perspective*

Children regularly explore more than one schema at a time. For this reason, worrying about identifying just the right one is less important than seeking multiple examples to enhance our understandings and ability to extend children's investigations.

In this chapter we offer a general definition of each schema and photos of children engaged in many examples of that schema. Then we share several stories that include photos and our reflections and questions. In our reflections we suggest thoughts about other schemas, name examples of brain development, and provide more ways to think about what is unfolding. We end each schema section with next steps to look for, think about, or try in your own work with children. Use our examples and stories to search for your own. Document what you uncover and put your head together with your colleagues' and families'. We can almost guarantee you will transform your teaching practices!

Transporting

With earnest intention, using an assortment of materials and equipment, children regularly take up the work of moving objects from one place to another. Once they get an object to a destination, they often do nothing with it. From our adult perspective, there seems to be no rhyme or reason as to why the children carry items from here to there. Yet when we observe the seriousness of their facial expressions, the purposeful stride of their body language, and the way they repeat these actions again and again, we can see these are not random acts. Our adult idea for *transporting* with the intent of accomplishing a specific task at a particular destination is very different from the children's points of view. Using vehicles like trucks and wagons, large and small containers, bags and purses, and cups and pitchers, the children are absorbed with the pure joy and satisfaction of moving objects and themselves. Study the photo examples to see if you recognize these repeated patterns, and read the stories that follow to hone your ability to see and appreciate the *transporting* schema.

Moving Big Blocks

Evan was immediately drawn to the big pile of large hollow blocks offered for building in the gym we use on rainy days. Deb was surprised when, rather than building or climbing, Evan proceeded to systematically move the blocks to the far side of the room. He worked diligently, pushing and carrying the heavy blocks, two at a time, until he had transported all the blocks to make another pile. Once he had moved them all, he ran off to find something else to do.

Is this experience one where two-year-old Evan's lively mind and active body were working together to build important concepts and brain connections? We could see the seriousness in his face and actions as the *transporting* schema called him to move every block across the room, with a deliberate yet varied approach. As he used his strength and balance to push and carry the heavy blocks, his brain sought input for his sensorimotor system. Evan's intuitive drive to *transport* the blocks is exactly in line with what is most useful for his development and learning. Before understanding schema play, Deb might have invited Evan to build something with the blocks. Rather than always following teachers' plans, it is fortunate that children are inspired to take up their own ideas, which may be far more impactful than what we design for them. Noticing the competence the children bring to their play, and allowing and extending their natural gifts (even when their actions confound us) is the role we want to play in children's learning.

From Here to There

Gaël and Gus were busy filling up their trucks with items from around the yard, gathering shovels, animals, buckets, bowls, and even big spools. These three-year-olds were proud and protective of their work—they each had their own truck to fill. They transported their trucks around the yard, collecting items, and then met up at the same spot to compare how much each had stockpiled. They complimented each other on the number of items they found and how much they were able to fit into their trucks. "Wow, you fit that big thing! I'm gonna get one too!"

Simultaneously, in another part of the yard, the five-year-olds were working on different ways to explore transporting. Alex, Henry, and Will took turns carrying each other in a big metal tub. Next they sat in trucks so Kyle could take them for a fast ride, stopping dangerously right at the edge of the sandbox. This was an exciting game! The children commented on his skills: "You push so fast, Kyle! Thanks for not pushing us into the sandbox!"

Gaël and Gus continued to transport their trucks around the yard, and then suddenly the classroom bell rang. "It's snacktime!" "Oh no!" "What will we do?" "Let's hide them!" They transported the trucks to the tunnel attached to the play structure and hid their trucks underneath. They giggled as they ran to their classroom together, pleased that their serious work was hidden and protected.

Reflections and Questions

Taking the time to pause and observe the children's work using schema theory as a lens, we see the significance and joy as the children collect and *transport* an abundance of materials using different methods. In this story, we can compare the way children of different ages use schema explorations. Having a mixed-age group provides children opportunities for collaboration and for the older children to model and help scaffold play. Teachers are able to see the children's many different strengths and skills.

We can also see how the children can engage in more than one schema exploration at the same time. The younger children have a clear goal: filling their trucks with as much as possible (*enclosing*)! They also use their strong bodies to push the trucks around the yard to different locations (*transporting*). As the children get older, the way they explore schemas becomes more complex and difficult. The five-year-olds transported each other and repeated this play in a variety of ways. The children also engaged with the thrill of the trajectory schema as they intentionally pushed with force to create speedy *transporting*. In all this work, we see the children's natural desire to move things or people from one place to another. This play also shows the children's cognitive skills and physical development: spatial awareness, comparing sizes and amounts, control of their bodies, turn taking, communication, and collaboration. This experience reminds us of the importance of offering children space, time, and a variety of items that they can use to *transport* from one place to another.

Your Turn

- Offer different materials for transporting to see what the children are drawn to.

- What details do you see, and how do the children explore the *transporting* schema?

- When observing what the children are doing, think about what the children's points of view may be.

- How do other teachers you work with understand this kind of play and learning? Do they think children are hoarding or being unsafe?

- How might you collaborate with your colleagues to better understand the importance of this type of play?

Transforming

Children engaged with the *transforming* schema almost always have a mesmerized look on their faces. They slow down to study the powerful changes they produce using paint, water, sand, or clay and building with open-ended materials. Spreading bright red and yellow paint over gleaming white paper is captivating for a baby newly experiencing the world of light and color. A small tray of water with a dry sponge invites children's curiosity and has so many possibilities for *transformation*. The water ripples and splashes when the children move it with their fingers. Their hands feel wet and cold as the water gleams and beads on their skin. Altering a large mound of playdough into many smaller balls is serious work to a preschool child. Older children are also fascinated and challenged by the power of *transforming* loose parts into intricate constructions or props for their dramas. Seeing the fascination of *transformation* through a child's eyes can remind adults of the world's wondrous possibilities. Yet the *transforming* schema can also be messy and annoying, particularly when it involves children squishing their food, covering their bodies in mud, or mixing the paint colors we so carefully set up for their art experiences. Study the photo examples here to see if you can recognize the magical moments, and then read the stories that follow to enhance your ability to see and join in with the children's amazement with the *transforming* schema.

Mesmerizing Transformations

The children were curious about the powdery white cornstarch filling the sensory table this week. It was soft and at the same time gritty to the touch. It could be patted, scooped, and spread around the table in its dry form. Just as appealing were the squeeze bottles filled with colored water. The children eagerly took up the satisfying task of squirting streams of water all over the cornstarch and watching the powerful transformation as the colorful water puddled and sank into the powder. Deb intentionally offered red water and yellow water so the children could observe the color change to gleaming orange. Mixing the watercolors and cornstarch transformed the consistency from a powder to an intriguing liquid that turned hard and dry when squeezed. Then it melted and dripped through the children's fingers when they opened their hands. The children used their lively, scientific minds to squirt and mix until every bit of the powder was changed. They were quiet and totally absorbed in this deep investigation.

Reflections and Questions

How does studying the children's full engagement with cornstarch help us see their point of view and the value of the *transformation* schema? Does the quest to *transform* offer the children a focused way of knowing and experiencing the world as they engage with their senses? How does the act of changing the cornstarch affect the children's feelings and thought processes as they explore the impact of their actions? As teachers we must keep revisiting the deeper meaning and value of *transforming* experiences. Offering children opportunities like this regularly takes energy and often courage. These materials are messy, requiring a lot of cleanup. The delight of goopy, squishy substances or the gratification of making a big muddle doesn't resonate with most adults. Honing observation skills to see the details of the world from children's perspectives can go a long way toward helping us appreciate the value of these experiences and even marvel with the children. From the initial dip of a finger into white powder to the total immersion of their hands in a colorful, silky substance, children teach us that life is meant to be experienced with our full attention.

Transformation Fascination

The children approached the table, eager to see the invitation of materials waiting for them. Nadia arranged containers filled with flour, salt, cream of tartar, and oil. "Nadia, what are we doing today?" the children asked. "We are making playdough!" Nadia responded as the children reacted with glee. "Yay!" "I want to help!" "Me too!" They all squeezed around the table and stood by for next steps. Nadia read the recipe out loud and designated jobs for all the children. They first mixed the dry ingredients. Mario volunteered to add the water. He carefully filled his measuring cup with water and poured it into the mix. Then came the most exciting part—the cooking and transforming! The children looked at the gooey liquid. Anjali asked, "How are we going to change it to playdough?" Nadia set up the skillet and gave each child a chance to stir and watch the transformation close up. "Oooooh!" "Aaaaaah!" "Wow!" The children were riveted as they saw the changes happening.

Reflections and Questions

Children enjoy mixing things together, whether it's their food at mealtime or paints at the easel. They are fascinated with seeing things *transform* from one state of matter to another. Understanding the power of the *transformation* schema can help teachers offer traditional activities, such as making playdough, with a new perspective. Inspired by this different window on cooking with children, Nadia was excited to work alongside them and experience the magic of *transformation*. She shared in the children's fascination as they watched how heat could completely change ingredients and turn them into something new. During this process the children used their scientific minds as they observed, predicted, and thought about physical science (changing forms from liquids to solid). They used mathematical thinking as they measured and counted how many scoops and cups were needed. They practiced literacy skills as they followed the recipe.

Nadia highlighted the children's interest by suggesting they describe the transformation of the ingredients as they observed it happening. Children naturally benefit from initiating their own schema investigations and working with teachers who guide their learning in a focused way. This experience was teacher planned and led, but Nadia considered how to meet up with the children's lively minds and fascination with the *transformation* schema.

The Goody Basket

The art area has become quite popular in our classroom of four- and five-year-olds. Children explore the variety of materials available and make all sorts of creations. Today Isabella approached a basket filled with recycled materials and noticed that it had been refilled with different-sized cardboard tubes and boxes. "Yay!" she exclaimed, hugging her new stuffed otter in one hand and digging through the basket with the other hand, gathering her favorite pieces. Isabella expertly used tape to attach cardboard tubes and boxes together to transform these ordinary materials into a creation that both she and her stuffed animal could use. She zoomed toward the front of the classroom and said, "Look at my scooter! My otter and I are going for a ride—see you later!" Isabella's creation inspired her friends, who jumped in to make other kinds of transporting machines.

Reflections and Questions

Even though our classroom has an abundance of open-ended materials to explore and create with, there is something about recycled materials that is different to children. Seeing the children's great interest in working with recycled materials, we decided to have a special basket for a collection of them. We named it the goody basket. Teachers and parents collect materials from their recycling bins at home and bring them in to share. We are astonished at the detailed and unique things the children make with cardboard, lids, caps, boxes, string, clips, and many other items. The children *connect* pieces together to *transform* them into masterpieces, using tape, glue, and string. Observing closely, we see that the children's goal is not necessarily just to create a masterpiece, but it is also to consider how to *connect* the pieces that challenges them. "How can I transform this material to be a part of my construction?" "How can I put these materials together?" "What would work best to keep them together?" "Which pieces will work best for my idea?" The goody basket has been in our classroom for over a year now. When we bring in new items to add to the basket, we wonder, "How will the children surprise us with their imagination and ingenuity today?"

Your Turn

If you don't already have a goody basket, collect some items to create one and offer it to children. Make sure you include different tools for connecting the items, and then observe what the children do.

- What is it about the materials that children love? What do they notice? How do they talk about what they are doing?

- How do children use the connecting and transforming schemas?

- What else can you offer the children to continue and extend this type of thinking and creativity?

Trajectory

Children find endless ways to propel objects and themselves. They are exhilarated when running, swinging, pushing, pulling, and launching themselves through the air. They love to make balls fly, cars zoom, and blocks crash, and even babies delight in watching their bottle fall as they drop it to the ground from their high chair. All of these movements are the core of the *trajectory* schema. Teachers find themselves regularly negotiating with children around *trajectory* explorations, as these actions can be dangerous and destructive. Yet this kind of movement is essential for children's development, and we should look for ways to invite children to explore this schema. Research shows that when children are prohibited from moving, they are likely to be clumsy, have difficulty paying attention, have trouble controlling their emotions, utilize poor problem-solving methods, and demonstrate struggles with social interactions (Hanscom 2016). Children's never-ending determination to move reflects the vital significance of these behaviors for brain development. Understanding the importance of children's actions can calm our fears and help us support children in their exploration of the *trajectory* schema with safety and purpose. Study the photos here to recognize the *trajectory* schema. As you read the longer stories, notice the children's body language and facial expressions that reflect the thrill and importance of moving.

A Jumping Game

Eighteen-month-old Wells eagerly seized the challenge of climbing up the big platform surrounded by pillows that Deb created for indoor active play. Standing at the top, Wells considered how she might get down. Jumping was a risky undertaking because the space between the platform and the pillows was too long and high up for her small toddler body. Wells seemed to immediately understand this, and instead she sat down on the edge of the platform and cautiously, yet bravely, propelled herself off, landing in the pillows. She popped up, exhilarated by this experience, and couldn't wait to do it again. She made her way back up the platform, sat on the edge, and, more exuberantly this time, flung herself onto the pillows. She did this over and over again, with joy and determination, inventing her own jumping game.

Reflections and Questions

The elation that comes from exploring the *trajectory* schema using their own bodies motivates even very young children like Wells to take risks that are vital to their learning and development. As we have come to recognize the fundamental connection between physical activity and brain development, we see the deeper significance of Wells's simple game. As she climbs and jumps, she is developing physical skills, including strength and balance. These actions also help build connections in her brain that support focus, attention, and self-regulation. As she invents and follows the sequence of her game, she is engaging in motor planning, which lays the foundation for other, more complex kinds of thinking and planning skills.

Adults often worry when children attempt physical risks. We instincively want to protect them, and for good reason. It is our job to keep them safe. However, Wells's initial, tentative leap off the platform shows us she is aware of and able to assess risks. From our many experiences observing children, we know that most often they know their limits and match their actions to their capabilities. From the time they are born, children are tenaciously focused on learning to move their bodies, so it follows that they must know a lot about their own physical abilities. We should always be alert to safety hazards, but we should also take time to see the children's skills and competencies before stepping in.

After testing the jump, Wells was confident that she could do it again. The exhilaration she felt from leaping off the platform and dropping heavily to the mat offered her satisfying, even calming, physical sensations. She was seeking proprioceptive input, and the jolt her body received from landing on the mat sent pleasing messages to her brain. We can see how her initiative to seek out *trajectory* experiences, her bravery, and her success brought Wells pride and satisfaction. These kinds of accomplishments will fortify her with self-confidence so she will eagerly take on more and more challenges in her life. We are dedicated to finding many ways for Wells and other children to engage in *trajectory* experiences and other physical challenges that will help them grow their physical skills and brain pathways.

The Physics of Trajectory

When the preschool boys saw the flat gray bins positioned near the slide, they all im-mediately shared the same idea—to ride one down the slide. The bins were a perfect fit for the width of the slide, so Garvey took the lead and arranged a bin at the top. He maneuvered his body to climb into the bin and prepared to go zooming down. To his surprise, he and the bin didn't move very fast, stalling just past the slope of the slide. Sawyer and Ryan tried it and suffered the same disappointing results. A renewed quest for speed began. The boys gave up getting inside and instead tried to get the bins to zoom down on their own. They had the idea that if they filled the bins with wood chips, the bins would go down faster. Their theory seemed to be that more weight would pro-pel the bins down. Big work began as the boys took up this idea and industriously filled the bins with wood chips. Each had their own bin and one by one placed the filled bins at the top of the slide, only to be disappointed again. They kept adding more wood chips and other objects, still believing that more weight would force the bins down. After many attempts, they changed plans and began joyfully using their arms and legs to push and pull, resulting in the speedy effects they were after.

Reflections and Questions

Self-initiated play experiences like this one are the most powerful way for children to learn about concepts like physics. The laws of physics cannot be taught to preschool children in a traditional lesson. Instead, their natural drive to explore the *trajectory* schema invites them to consider physics concepts like motion, speed, velocity, weight, gravity, and angle. They experience these concepts with their bodies and minds, sharing perspectives and collaborating on the task. We marvel at the children's innate drive to explore how the world works, and we let them know this too: "You are skillful scientists observing closely and experimenting to learn about the physics of gravity, speed, and motion." Teachers have learned these physics terms and their meanings so we can be informative with the children. We can also look for more ways to provision materials so children may continue with these kinds of explorations.

The Surprise Catapult

As Gavin reached down to get his long-handled shovel, he accidentally stepped on the handle. To his surprise, his actions made a small plastic ball fly high into the air. He had unintentionally created a catapult. Gavin was extremely thrilled with this discovery and called over his friend Nayan to show him. This time he carefully set up the shovel at the edge of the sandbox, put the ball on the end of it, and then stomped as hard as he could. The ball zoomed up into the air! The boys cheered, "Let's do it again!" Nayan ran to get his own supplies, and they set up their shovels side by side. An audience of children and adults gathered and together called out, "Ready, set, go!" Gavin and Nayan stomped on the handles, and the balls went flying. They eagerly chased after them to do it all over again!

Reflections and Questions

In this moment of discovery, Nadia was as excited as the children. From the children's point of view, what a wonderful feeling it must be to take complete delight in your work and proudly share it with your friends and teachers. Also notable are the skills and competencies Gavin used to figure out what made the ball fly and how he could re-create that moment to coach his friend. The children in the audience watched with admiration as the boys used all the force they could muster to stomp on the shovel. The impact of their actions electrified them as the balls went hurtling up into the air!

Children have the natural urge to throw and drop things. We have learned that finding different ways to make this happen is an important part of children's exploration of the *trajectory* schema. Now that the children have discovered this new way to make things fly, we wonder what might come next.

Your Turn

- What have you seen children do to make things fly and move with speed and force?

- What are your reactions to children's use of the trajectory schema? Why?

- Does understanding the underlying importance of trajectory explorations deepen your views?

- How might you negotiate your concerns for children's safety with the vital explorations children must engage in to develop their brains?

- What materials might you offer to encourage trajectory schema explorations in safe, complex ways? Try them out and study what unfolds.

Rotation and Circularity

Children delight in spinning until they are dizzy, rolling down hills, and joyously running and dancing around. They also have a strong interest in exploring wheels, balls, knobs, and anything else that can be rolled, turned, twirled, twisted, or spun. They enjoy seeing and creating curved lines and circles. These are all reflections of the *rotation* and *circularity* schemas.

Why are children so drawn to these schemas? Body movements that involve spinning and rolling call on the vestibular system, which helps children develop the brain pathways for balance and spatial awareness. Children enjoy and intuitively understand the importance of moving in this way for their development.

An abundance of research suggests that a preference for circular shapes is deeply ingrained in all of us from birth. One study found that at five months of age, babies show a clear visual preference for contoured lines over straight lines. Using brain imaging, scientists can see portions of the brain light up when a subject is looking at particular shapes. When looking at edges and sharp lines, the parts of the brain responsible for fear, anxiety, and aggressiveness light up. When people look at *circles* and curved shapes, the areas of the brain that foster feelings of calm and safety light up. Other studies looked at how the shapes in faces display certain emotions. They discovered that smiling faces take on a *circular* shape, while frowning and angry faces are triangular shaped (Lima 2017). It's no wonder children are enamored with circles and spinning. Examine the photos and stories here to think more about how and why children pursue the *rotation* and *circularity* schemas.

Dancing around with Elephants

With watering cans shaped like elephants in hand, two-year-old Dylan and Annette followed each other around the path of the play yard. At one point they began to drag the elephant trunks on the ground, noticing and delighting in the scraping sound they were making together. A new discovery emerged as they spotted drops of water coming from the elephant trunks. They joined together to spin around and around, touching the trunks to the ground, creating the scuffling sound and closely inspecting the flying drops and the circular marks created in the sand by their movement with the cans.

Reflections and Questions

This was such a seemingly serendipitous moment between the children, and yet contemplating the *rotation* and *circularity* schemas helps us understand the more significant underlying forces influencing Dylan and Annette's play. The children's minds and bodies immediately met to share this magical connection around *rotation* and *circularity*. Using their open and flexible brains to pick up on every sound and trace of their movements, their attention was drawn to the circles scraped in the sand and their own *rotating* bodies. Were they revisiting their *rotating* movements by studying the marks left on the ground? The children's *circling* movements were in sync as they danced around each other with excitement. From our research on schema theory as well as our observation of other human experiences, we can see the influence of the children's attention to *rotation* and *circularity* in their play. We marvel at this powerful moment in the children's friendship and learning and are grateful that we can understand the significance as we witness it.

Ready, Set, Go!

A marvelous collaboration unfolded in the yard today. William was at the top of the slide holding on to a big red bouncy ball, and Diane was positioning one at the bottom. Isabella filled the space in between with more balls. Carrick surprised Nadia when she saw him hiding under the first ball at the top. She realized he was waiting to launch the balls down the slide. Together the children counted down: "Five, four, three, two, one, go!" With anticipation, Carrick gave a big push and slid down as the balls tumbled down with him. The children cheered and screamed with delight as something unexpected happened: the balls started flying off the side of the slide! They enthusiastically decided to try it again. More children took notice, eager to watch the show. They took turns with the different tasks to continue the game. For the next run, Diane arranged the balls at the top, Carrick held the balls at the bottom of the slide, and William squeezed balls into the middle. This time it was Isabella's turn to slide down. "Ready, set, go!" As she sped down, the balls rolled with her, flying off the slide again. Children waited eagerly for a turn, and soon many more had joined this rousing game!

Reflection and Questions

The game the children invented was a new and surprising way to use these big balls. Our adult reaction is often to question how children use materials: "Shouldn't the children be sitting on the balls and bouncing around, as the balls are intended to be used?" When we respond to children's ideas from this prescribed view, we often impose rules that, with more reflection, seem unnecessary and limiting to the children's experiences. For several years, the educators in our school have been reflecting on ideas about the "rules" we impose on children's use of materials. We have come to appreciate the children's flexible, creative thinking, because we take time to observe their play with openness and curiosity. Now we are fascinated by how they come up with these extraordinary ideas.

What did the children notice and think about as they invented this game? Did their attraction to the *rotation* and *circularity* schemas inspire them? There was an abundance of the round, heavy balls, and they were almost the same size as the children. To roll with the balls down the ramp required complex thinking, skillful physical maneuvers, and collaboration. *Orientation* and *positioning* schema explorations were involved as the children placed the balls in just the right way to move in conjunction with the movement of their bodies. The *trajectory* schema also added big thrills to the game as the giant balls flew down and off the slide.

Creative thinking and inventing come naturally to children. It is the way they live and learn. As we get older, we are often invested in doing things the "right way." We wonder how to get back our ability to think as these young children do, so we make sure we recognize and help their remarkable learning abilities grow.

Your Turn

- What is your reaction to how the children used the balls in the game they invented?

- What details did you hear that show the children's skills and competence? What schemas can you identify in this game?

- If you try to put yourself in the children's shoes, how might you describe this experience? How do the children in your group use rotation and circularity schemas?

Enclosing and Enveloping

Children seem to have a spiritual quest to fill a hole or climb into a cozy space. It is impossible to count the number of times we have seen children *enclose* cups, bowls, and containers with nearby objects or climb into boxes, cupboards, tents, or other small spaces. Children use blocks to build *enclosures* for toy animals or themselves, they completely cover playdough (*envelope*) with gems, or they draw a border around a painting. Children drape fabrics over objects and furniture, and a toddler will put any open container on their head. These are all part of the *enclosing* and *enveloping* schemas. What may be the underlying reasons for these schemas? Most obvious is that children are learning how their bodies and other objects fit into the spaces around them. This develops spatial reasoning, which is critical for negotiating yourself in space, as well as learning math skills. Also, filling a hole must be extremely satisfying to children, like completing a jigsaw puzzle is to an adult. The fact that they can fit something perfectly into a space offers a sense of mastery and gratification.

The world is big and children are small, so maybe the appeal of spending time in a small, cozy space helps children feel safe. *Enclosing* and *enveloping* could also provide children with input to their proprioceptive system, which sends calming signals to the brain. Hugging and swaddling, which affects the proprioceptive system, have long been used to soothe a crying baby. Could children be offering this comfort to themselves through *enveloping* and *enclosing*? What thoughts do you have as you study the photos here of children exploring the *enclosing* and *enveloping* schemas? Enjoy the stories that follow to learn more.

Where Have All the Teddy Bears Gone?

Several children from the three-year-old classroom came to visit Nadia's five-year-olds this morning. Emnet and Isha went straight to the dramatic play area, their favorite space in any classroom! They put on as many dress-up clothes as they possibly could and then looked in the mirror together and laughed hysterically. Next they put on fancy shoes and industriously filled up purses with cameras, phones, food, and doctor tools. Meanwhile, Gus and Yaseen explored the light projector. Yaseen lined up the transparent teddy bears and other animals, and then put some of them in small transparent boxes. Gus took a handful of the animals to the small rug in the Lego area. He carefully arranged the animals on a toy car. Emnet and Isha came over to see what their friends were doing. When Yaseen and Gus saw them dressed up in so many layers holding overflowing purses, they laughed and joined them in their dress-up game. The children spent thirty minutes together, dressing each other, filling up purses, and walking around the classroom holding baby dolls. When it was time to leave, they put the materials away as best they could and went back to their classroom.

Later that day, five-year-olds Ann and Lea went to work at the light projector. They noticed that all the new teddy bears were gone! They searched everywhere and could not find them. It was a mystery! The following week, the children set up a tea party in the dramatic play area. They dressed up for the occasion and chose purses. They soon announced to the classroom, "We found them! The teddy bears! They are in all the purses!" The children and teachers had a good laugh, knowing it was their three-year-old friends whose passion for filling every bag and purse was the source of the mystery.

Reflections and Questions

When designing the classroom environment, we pay close attention to the skills and interest of five-year-olds. We carefully choose materials that can provide a challenge and opportunities for complex, open-ended play. This school year, the younger children have been frequent visitors to our classroom. We welcome them with open arms and have been astonished to see them use the space and materials so competently. We closely observe their work and see many schema explorations in their play. They do a lot of *transporting*, *positioning*, and *transforming*. The schemas we have found most fascinating are *enveloping* and *enclosing*. It can be frustrating when we look for our favorite items, and then have a good laugh when we find purses and bags stuffed with these random materials days after the younger children have left. Schema theory offers teachers aha moments, because it helps us understand that young children have a need to fill an empty space. Knowing that these repeated behaviors help children build important brain connections, we are more intentional about the materials we provide in our classrooms. We are always on the lookout for opportunities for *enveloping* and *enclosing* by providing loose parts and purses, backpacks, bowls, boxes, and trucks. Along with the five-year-olds, we now delight in the mystery of finding items the three-year-old children have *enveloped* and *enclosed* each day. The five-year-olds understand and appreciate that this is the way their younger friends play and learn.

Tiny Holes

The toddlers used fierce concentration in the studio today as they approached the tricky task of inserting pushpins through very tiny holes in wooden shapes and into a corkboard. Deb offered a commercial hammering toy meant for older children, because she had seen the group's interest in using real tools. Instead, the children—eighteen- to twenty-four-month-olds—surprised her again when they were much more interested in the challenge of using their fine-motor skills, rather than the hammering toy, to fit the pins in the small holes. It took deliberation and effort for them just to pick up the pins, and it was even more difficult for the children to fit the pins into the minuscule holes of the wooden shapes. The children used many strategies to steady their hands and focus their eyes as they worked. Some held the wooden pieces up to their faces to take a closer look. Others held on to the pieces with one hand to steady them on the corks while they put the pins in the holes. The children carefully decided where there was enough space to add a new wooden shape to the corkboard. The quiet intensity of their work permeated the studio. Several children stayed with this task for over forty minutes.

Reflections and Questions

We marvel at the children's strong drive and persistence to work with a challenge, which many people believe are beyond their years and skills. Some may even think the pokey pins are too risky and worry about the children getting hurt. Instead, we ponder what is so enticing to the children about filling the small holes with the pins. We know that *enclosure* explorations are compelling to children, but their attention to this work is more complex. Is it because the task is such an enormous challenge for them? Do the children have an inherent tenacity to engage in novel experiences? Current brain research says this is true. Children are continually attracted to new materials and environments and will find multiple ways to learn with them. What dispositions and skills do you see the children learning as they fill the holes with pins?

Bath Time

Nadia wanted to involve the children in cleaning out buckets that were coated with some kind of dried chalk goo left over from an earlier experiment. She set up an invitation of big metal tubs filled with soapy water and brushes. A group of three-year-old children happily accepted the invitation to scrub the buckets. She left them to do the work independently. When Nadia returned with more buckets and shovels that needed to be cleaned, she was in for a big surprise. The children were no longer washing the buckets. They were washing themselves! With big smiles on their faces, the children took turns squeezing into the bin two at a time. The children covered their bodies with chalk and used the brushes to scrub it off their legs and arms.

Reflection and Questions

After taking a moment to reflect, Nadia laughed. What was she thinking? Of course it was much more fun to wash yourself! The children were completely *enveloped* in this sensory experience of warm soapy water and brushes on their bodies. We have seen children determined to build barriers around animals or create *enclosures* in their drawings. In this story, the metal tub served as an *enclosure* around their bodies as they were *enveloped* by the sudsy water. This experience was a reminder of how children's brains work and empower them to see all the different possibilities in materials.

Your Turn

Consider these questions as you observe and plan for children's *enclosing* and *enveloping* schema explorations.

- What opportunities can we offer children to explore enclosing and enveloping?
- How do the children show us the importance of this kind of play?
- What is our role as teachers when children use materials in different ways than we intend? Is it okay to sometimes say no?

Connecting and Disconnecting

Children are brilliant learners, able to try out ideas and consolidate understandings as they investigate the world around them. One of the essential strategies they use is to put things together and take them apart, studying how materials can be linked and their relationships to one another, through the *connecting* and *disconnecting* schemas. The urge to *connect* and *disconnect* materials is seen as children play with train sets, Legos, magnet tiles, and other building toys. Children using this schema will also be fascinated with joining things together using materials such as tape, glue, string, or ribbon. We have watched even our youngest children spend days mastering the use of tape. When we coach preschoolers in using glue guns, they are ecstatic over the *connecting* power this new skill offers. Children enjoy tying or wrapping string around objects and furniture or connecting rope or a leash to their stuffed animals to walk them around the room. Layering and stacking objects is also reflected in this schema. Children will stack and balance blocks or stones or pile layers of objects on top of each other.

Disconnecting is as engaging to children as *connecting*. Tearing things apart, crashing block structures, and scattering objects is exciting for children yet often exasperating to adults. Another version of the *connecting* and *disconnecting* schemas is assembling and disassembling. Children will gather materials and pile them all together, and then just as joyfully demolish the pile. We have heard teachers humorously call these "learning piles," trying to give the children's quest for creating giant piles more meaning.

Understanding the importance of schema play helps us realize that all these activities encourage children's development. Through *connecting* and *disconnecting,* scattering, assembling, and disassembling, children develop problem-solving skills, understand cause and effect, practice classification, and learn how to use tools safely and effectively. Look for these schemas in the photos and study the stories to enhance your understanding of these fascinating and sometimes frustrating activities children pursue.

"I'm Making a Package!"

The children are regularly interested in our creation station, an area of the classroom that offers many recycled and natural loose parts with tools and materials for constructing. Three-year-old Yveline has been particularly focused on learning to use the tape from the creation station. She has been practicing unrolling the tape, using scissors to cut pieces, and then placing the pieces carefully on paper to make a design. This is a tricky task, but her practice has paid off. Today she decides to use her new skills to do something more challenging. She folds the edges of the paper over, and then little by little cuts pieces of tape and uses them to tape down the edges of the paper. As she works, she talks about what she is doing. "I'm making a package. I'm going to give this to my mommy and daddy, and they will say, 'Oh, thank you.'" She studies her creation, and then with a big grin announces, "When they open it, they will say, 'Oh no, there's nothing inside!'" She laughs uproariously as she imagines this surprising moment.

Reflections and Questions

Tape and the other materials in our creation station are useful for *connecting* and *disconnecting* schema explorations. As a toddler, Yveline loved to use pieces of tape just to stick and unstick, over and over again, to a variety of surfaces. She has been using tape in this fascinating and challenging way to explore the *connecting* and *disconnecting* schemas for many years. When she was younger, Deb needed to help her tear off the pieces of tape, as this task was difficult for her motor skills. Now that she is three, she is determined to master these skills for herself and is gratified to be able to cut pieces of tape to actually make something. We see a big leap in her development as she understands that she can use the tape to *connect* the paper together to make a present for her family. She has a purposeful plan for using the *connecting* schema that she has been intuitively exploring and coming to understand for so long. Her sense of humor and ability to take other perspectives shine through as she notes that her package is empty and cheerfully predicts how her family will respond. Has Yveline's simple schema play over the years helped her build these more complex understandings? She is now able to use her skills and knowledge of *connecting* to make a product of her own design. We also wonder if Yveline's experiences of *enclosing* herself and other objects prompts her to delight in the package being empty. We have studied humor in young children and have come to understand that they believe something is funny if it does not fit the ordinary patterns of everyday life. Certainly being offered the gift of an empty package fits that notion. Observing and analyzing the details of Yveline's remarkable instincts about what she needs to do for her growth and development reinforces our practice to continue noticing, allowing, and planning opportunities for her to lead the way.

Scattering Sticks

The children in Deb's toddler room turned two and were ready for more challenging activities. Deb decided to offer them K'NEX, a commercial toy that requires keen eye-hand coordination. The children took up this new appealing task, working diligently to snap the pieces together. The materials were spread over the tabletop, which sparked a new idea in Annette. Slowly, she moved a few pieces to the edge of the table, pushing them until they fell to the ground. Then she looked up sheepishly at Deb, who smiled at her. Annette's new idea immediately resonated with Evan and Kahaan, and they began scattering the pieces all over the table, watching them fly off. The children's excitement grew as they swiped at more and more pieces until they all sailed off. Evan and Kahaan added complexity to the game by using sticks as tools to fling pieces to the ground. The children swung and wacked at the pieces until the table was completely bare. Then they took the game to the floor, again using sticks to scatter the pieces all over the room.

Reflections and Questions

Finding out that scattering is a version of the *connecting* and *disconnecting* schemas makes the children's behavior in this story just a little more tolerable. In these moments, Deb would rather the children not make toys fly all over the room. It feels wild, disrespectful to the materials, and maybe even unsafe. Yet because children explore the world in this way so often, it invites more reflection. Why is scattering and flinging materials so interesting to children? What could be the importance of this work? Perhaps the children feel powerful when they make the materials fly so far and fast. They are exploring physics and mathematical concepts like gravity and velocity. The chaos and unpredictability of where the objects will land is fascinating and exciting. Because this sort of behavior is often stopped, maybe children relish the concerned responses adults have when they do it. The adult's reaction seemed to be part of Annette's goal when she looked up for Deb's reaction. But Annette often pushes toys and materials off of countertops and shelves without looking for approval, so something more than just testing her power with adults was going on for her.

Adults don't have to love these explorations, but we can understand the importance of the children's innate desire to investigate in big ways, to observe the cause and effect of their actions. During this endeavor, the children showed us their scientific minds as they engaged in a physics experiment. We admired their brilliant, flexible thinking as they added complexity to the game by inventing tools to make their work more challenging.

As reflective teachers, we pause to consider what is unfolding, especially in spicy situations. We ask ourselves, what are the possible meanings we can make of this experience? How are the children showing us their competence and perspective? We may stop an activity that seems destructive or unsafe but then ask ourselves what we can do to meet up with the children's minds to enhance their skills.

We now plan activities where the children can scatter to their hearts' content, and we are okay with it. How could you offer children opportunities to do the exhilarating work of scattering that would be okay with you?

Miles and Caleb's Idea

Miles came to sit at the table, where an invitation of playdough and various loose parts awaited him. He began by forming many balls with the playdough. When he was done, he left the table to explore the ramp set in the block area. He seemed to be on a mission as he looked at the different sizes of tubes and ramps. He carried a big cardboard tube to the dollhouse and put it through the rooftop window. He came back to the table to gather the balls of dough. Then he placed the playdough balls on the tube and used them as a way to connect animals and people along the tube. He invited Caleb to join his play. They collaborated, adding more items to be connected using playdough, and were excited about what they could do next. "Let's put furniture on it too! And more bugs!" They were proud to work together on this new idea.

Reflection and Questions

In the mornings, we often set up open-ended, tactile experiences. Having something to touch and *transform* can be very soothing, particularly after saying goodbye to a parent. Teacher Nadia set up an invitation for children to explore playdough with a variety of loose parts. Little did she know that Miles and Caleb would have a completely unique idea. She was extremely curious about what they were doing. It was not typical for children to take playdough from the table. Nadia almost stopped them but decided to wait to see their idea. Miles and Caleb used a variety of materials to make an amazing creation. They brilliantly used the playdough as a glue to *connect* the animals to the tube. These children are innovators! They never create the same thing twice. Every day their work is a surprise. Children like Miles and Caleb teach us to be patient, to be flexible, and to appreciate the many possibilities of schema explorations when we offer open-ended materials. We see children do things that we would never imagine. And to think, Nadia almost stopped them from doing it!

Your Turn

- How does this experience support the idea that children use schemas as a way to figure out the world around them? In this case, did you see the theories and predictions the children explored about how these materials could work together?

- What other materials and opportunities could Nadia offer Miles and Caleb to engage in new and unique experiences in connecting and disconnecting?

- How did the boys' ideas challenge or support your thinking about how children use materials?

Positioning and Ordering

Young children are constantly figuring out about the world by noticing similarities and differences and sorting and classifying everything. They are doing this with people, other living creatures, and objects. The *positioning* and *ordering* schemas, where children sort, classify, and carefully place objects in lines, patterns, sequences, and groups, have deepened our understanding of the remarkable gifts children possess for learning.

In our daily work, we are often astonished by children's attention to *order*, beauty, and aesthetically pleasing designs in their play with materials. The elements of creative design used by artists seem to be inherently at work in children's *positioning* and *ordering* explorations. As we study children's efforts and attempt to meet up with their minds, we see that they intuitively and intentionally notice color, shape, line, size, pattern, texture, space, form, unity, and balance in their *positioning* and *ordering* work (Brommer 2010).

We marvel at children carefully placing objects in patterns or rows. We can see it as children line up toys, books, or other objects and *position* them either on top of, under, around, behind, or next to each other. The children *order* objects according to size, color, or shape. They also arrange beautiful collections of loose parts, decorate playdough and their block structures, and create patterns and rows when painting or drawing. Take time to pause and wonder at the photos we have offered here, and then read the stories of the complex work children do while using the *positioning* and *ordering* schemas. See if you can identify the elements of design in the photos and descriptions of the children's work.

Jeffrey's Precise Work

Today two-year-old Jeffrey's explorations were an example of the fascinating way he approaches play all the time. The plastic eggs and containers on the table caught his attention. He was particularly drawn to the broken egg with a hole in it. He proceeded to slowly and meticulously tear the egg apart, piece by piece, arranging the shells perfectly on top of each other to fit the opening in the container. Once he had finished this task, he spread the shell pieces in front of him on the table, examined them very closely, and then again purposefully placed them in the tray. Jeffrey's hands were graceful as he used extraordinarily steady hand-eye coordination while he worked. It seemed as if he were moving in super slow motion. He paused to notice each aspect of his work, examining the materials and contemplating his actions until he was satisfied with the results. He spent at least twenty minutes at this task.

Reflections and Questions

We strongly value taking care of our materials and usually remind children to use them respectfully. Deb didn't intervene in Jeffrey's undertaking because his work was remarkable and his interest intense, and because the egg was already broken. Jeffrey was obviously not involved in random or destructive play during this experience. We can see the intention in his work and should consider the deeper, internal, and specifically directed thoughts, abstract ideas, patterns, and concepts Jeffrey was investigating. Jeffrey was attracted to many schemas in this experience. The *positioning* and *ordering* schemas seemed most central to his work. He carefully tore off pieces of the egg and then, just as intentionally, placed them impeccably on top of one another. Then he *positioned* them in a different way by spreading them in front of himself on the table. He reordered the eggshells again by placing them on top of each other in the container. He intensely studied the *transformation* of the egg as he took it apart. He enjoyed *connecting* and *disconnecting* the shells, stacking and unstacking them, piece by piece. And he felt gratified as he *enclosed* the egg pieces in the container as he *transported* them back and forth from the table to the container. Jeffrey's precision, exceptional fine-motor skills, and serious disposition lead us to think that someday he might be a brain surgeon. What do you think? How would you further support Jeffrey's interest in *positioning* and *ordering*?

My Pumpkin Patch

Ben came to the table and immediately began to manipulate the kinetic sand and spread it out carefully with his hands. He studied the trays of small acrylic pumpkins, corks, and wooden rings. He began picking up pumpkins one at a time and pushing them into the sand. He thoughtfully placed the pumpkins next to one another in several rows. Next he lined up a few rows of acorns. His finishing touch was positioning a wall of corks. Ben felt satisfied with his work, looked up to see if anyone was nearby, and announced in a proud voice, "Who wants to come see my pumpkin patch?"

Reflections and Questions

We are captivated by Ben's attention to detail and his eye for design in this work. As he carefully lines up the pumpkins and other materials, Ben is exploring the *positioning* and *ordering* schemas. We are often impressed by the beauty of children's designs, like Ben's play in this story. Children's careful attention to shape, size, color, and texture as they arrange materials is as pleasing to our senses as it is to theirs. As we observe children's use of the *ordering* and *positioning* schemas, we learn the kinds of materials that will provoke this creative work. We have come to think of our offerings as gifts to meet up with children's amazing brains. In this collection of materials, the kinetic sand is a powerful material for sensory investigation, as children can *transform* it in many ways. Ben uses the sand as a base for his design, arranging and rearranging it to support his unfolding ideas. The other loose parts are open-ended, sparkly, and colorful, and have many shapes and textures. The materials speak to Ben, inviting him to study their properties, deciding how they are alike and different, and using this information to plan his creation. Embedded in this schema play, Ben is also exploring math concepts such as sorting, classifying, and exploring magnitude. Searching for materials, offering these treasures to children, and seeing them use them in marvelous ways is one of the most satisfying aspects of our work as teachers.

Your Turn

Use the following questions to invite your children to explore beauty and design through the *ordering* and *positioning* schemas:

- What items do you already have in your room that draw the children to explore *ordering* and *positioning*?
- How do the children use the properties of these materials in their *ordering* and *positioning* work?
- What other materials and activities can you offer children to explore the *ordering* and *positioning* schemas? Search the natural world, thrift stores, and art stores for interesting loose parts to use. Observe how the children use them to help yourself learn more.

Orientation and Perspective

Children see more, hear more, and experience the world more fully than adults. Their brains are in the process of making connections that help them make sense of the multisensory world surrounding them. No wonder they inherently use the *orientation* and *perspective* schemas to grow these understandings. Children continually find ways to look at things from different viewpoints. To understand the world from many perspectives, children play with *perception* and *orientation* and place themselves in a number of interesting positions. They may climb up high or spend time lying on the floor, viewing the world sideways. They may look through their legs or hang upside down from a climbing structure. They also put objects or themselves in different places and positions. Hiding under furniture, hanging upside down, or looking out from a high climber or platform are actions that are all part of the *orientation* and *perspective* schemas. Children also continually put objects up to their eyes, peer through a magnifying glass or a translucent piece of fabric, or look closely in a mirror. We continually wonder at and delight in the children's points of view, as we know they see the world so differently than we do. As you study the photos and read the stories here, see what you can discover about children's exploration of the *orientation* and *perspective* schemas.

Playing with Sunshine

The gift of sunshine on this cold winter morning brought joy to everyone in the toddler yard today. Deb was inspired to invite more attention to the light by hanging colorful cellophane and sparkly beads from the metal arches. The children eagerly took up the invitation to envelope themselves in the magic. They delighted in the vibrant world they became a part of as they wrapped themselves in the hangings. They also stopped to study the movement and sounds their actions created. The children were especially joyful when they could see each other through the translucent materials. They didn't rush through the barrier. Instead, they moved slowly, alert to the full engagement of their senses—what they could see, hear, and especially feel as the shiny beads and crinkly paper flowed over their heads and bodies. They had dreamy looks on their faces and returned again and again to the experience.

Reflections and Questions

What might the children's points of view be during these moments as they hear, see, and experience things more deeply than we do? Sharing in this experience can remind us of the wonders the world offers. This isn't just a simple sensory experience; it is also a reflection of aesthetic development. Aesthetics is a branch of philosophy dealing with the nature of beauty on the earth. Sensory experiences are input to the brain, and aesthetic experiences are our emotional and intellectual responses to that input. We liken it to the enormous feelings we have when we see a beautiful sunset over the ocean and ponder what it means about life. We love thinking about these moments with the children as a study in aesthetics, of beauty on the earth, and feeling and sharing the thrill of that beauty fully in our minds and bodies.

The *orientation* and *perspective* schemas seem to be essential to this experience for the children. They seek to see the world in new ways, and the beads and cellophane give them a magical way to do this. Again, we wonder how the children's ongoing quest to be *enveloped* in experiences and to *transform* themselves and the world around them provoke and sustain this play. How do dancing with the beads and *enveloping* themselves in the many sensory aspects of this environment affect the development of the children's sensorimotor systems and their brains and ultimately shape their *perspective* of the world? Being able to see and appreciate multiple perspectives is a critical aspect of getting along in our very diverse world.

We Did It!

Ann and Lea are not newcomers to the monkey bars. In fact, they have been frequent visitors for the last two years. One might even call them experts. Building on these many years of experience, Lea discovered a new way to use her body today. She lifted herself up and did a backward spin. "How do you do that?" Ann asked. Lea described and modeled it for her, repeating the spinning actions many times. Ann kept trying but was not able to spin. Lea encouraged her, "You just have to keep practicing!" A few minutes later, Ann squealed with excitement, "I did it! Lea, look. I did it!" After spinning several times, Ann felt confident and suggested they create a new game. "After we flip, let's play a clapping game!" The new game involved hanging upside down while playing patty cake.

This inspired other children to create games while hanging from the monkey bars and other climbing structures. "Let's touch foreheads after we flip!" Lola invited Ari, and she was ready for the challenge. They worked carefully to coordinate their movements to avoid crashing their heads together. It took several tries, but soon they announced, "We did it!" There was a lot of excitement and cheering from friends and, of course, the invention of more games.

Reflections and Questions

This remarkable play on the monkey bars shows children exploring the *orientation* and *perspective* schemas. Taking on these unique and risky moves was not easy work. Nadia was worried that the children might hurt themselves as their heads hit. But as she watched, she saw the children had the strength and flexibility to lift themselves up, hang in different positions, and skillfully spin and flip their bodies to gain these exhilarating *perspectives*. They understood they had to communicate clearly and agree on the rules, all this while synchronizing their bodies—upside down! No wonder they were so excited when they succeeded with these risky experiments. The children also explored the *trajectory* and *rotation* schemas as their bodies moved rapidly around and around.

As adults, we rarely move our bodies in these ways anymore. What does it feel like to be able to *orient* your body to gain a new *perspective* on what is happening around you? Engaging in this play certainly builds new connections in the children's brains as they jubilantly explore multiple *perspectives* with their bodies and each other.

Your Turn

- Observe your group of children, looking for the ways they try to explore different *orientations* and new *perspectives*. Try out what you see them doing to get a new view of the world.

- What new thinking or feelings do you have from these experiences? How does this help you meet up with the children's minds?

- How can you find ways in your own adult life to engage with the *orientation* and *perspective* schemas?

- Why do you think it is important to be able to take multiple perspectives?

CHAPTER 3

Schema Explorations—A Strong Force in Children's Learning and Development

Our understandings of children's use of schema explorations has fortified our belief that children naturally do what they need to do for their learning and development. Children use schemas everywhere, and we have come to recognize that schemas motivate and support children's learning in many domains. We have observed children using schema play to do the following:

- drive active play for healthy brain development
- invite social connections and collaboration
- build math skills
- enhance art explorations
- advance scripts for imaginative play
- extend long-term investigations

This chapter offers stories of play in each of these domains and our reflections and understandings of how schema explorations are essential to furthering all aspects of children's development.

Schemas Drive Active Play for Healthy Brain Development

Along with our study of schema theory, we have been reading research about the connection between active play and brain development. As children are constantly engaged in schema explorations, they are also endlessly moving. When children move their bodies, staying healthy and practicing physical skills aren't the only benefits. Active play while using schemas is essential for sensorimotor development. This kind of play actually builds the neural pathways necessary for children to focus their eyes and attention, regulate their emotions, and develop the ability to plan and carry out a task (Hanscom 2016).

Using both of these lenses, we see how active play and schema explorations are fundamentally connected. *Enclosing* themselves in a cardboard box, *transporting* a bucket of sand, or playing with *trajectory* as they fly down a slide, children continually use their bodies to explore schemas. Learning more about the connection between active play and brain development has helped us realize the significance of movement in children's schema explorations. For example, *trajectory*, *rotation*, and *transporting* engage the vestibular sense. The vestibular sense is a complex system located in our inner ear and consists of gravity receptors that detect linear movements, such as running straight or swinging back and forth, and rotary or spinning movements. The vestibular system helps us know where our bodies are in space. It helps us keep our balance and make sure that we are safe in our environment.

Enclosing and *enveloping* call on the proprioceptive sense, which provides input and feedback that tells us about movement and body position. Its "receptors" are located within our muscles, joints, ligaments, tendons, and connective tissues.

When children don't have the opportunity to move, their brain development suffers and results in underdeveloped proprioceptive and vestibular systems. Children with these underdeveloped systems may be clumsy, uncoordinated, and unable to regulate their emotions, and they may have difficulty performing basic childhood tasks and activities (Hanscom 2016).

A bulk of our time as early childhood educators is spent negotiating with children around active play and movement. School readiness agendas that emphasize sitting and listening to learn, environmental rating scales that focus on requiring special areas and materials for academic skills, and an increased attention on safety and risk avoidance have led to fewer opportunities for children to be active. When teachers work to prevent or stop children from moving, rather than plan for it, children suffer. We need to understand that children's natural interest in moving their bodies through schema explorations ensures that their brains are developing the connections that are essential to the rest of their lives. We are fiercely passionate about supporting children in their efforts to move. Read the following stories that reflect our experiences and thinking.

Is Dylan Learning to Read?

Recently Dylan's mom shared with Deb that she was a little worried eighteen-month-old Dylan doesn't spend much time looking at books. Today Deb noticed that "looking" was only one way Dylan was spending time with a book. In the midst of driving the green truck up and down the ramp, he stopped when he noticed a book. Stretched out, flat on his belly, Dylan studied photos of his friend Madeline in her portfolio book. Next, seeking a different perspective, he got up on his feet and bent over, leaning in close and balancing as he studied the page. Moving his body to a squat and then to a sitting position, he spent quite a bit of time manipulating the book. He examined the cover and the pages, searching for how it was put together. Finally, he tried to take the book apart. He worked to open the binder rings, and he examined the texture of the plastic sleeves and how they changed and moved in response to his actions. Dylan was totally immersed in the book for more than fifteen minutes.

Reflections and Questions

Dylan brings his body with him in everything he does. He thrives on physical activity, seeking to move all day long. His encounter with the book is a perfect example of this. Current brain research suggests that when children are moving, they are more able to be focused and calm. Motor planning—thinking about how to move our bodies—is the foundation for other kinds of thinking and planning skills. When children move, they process sensory information and practice appropriate responses to the environment around them. Mastering their bodies leads to skills and behavior for focused attention and self-regulation, allowing children to control their physical activity, emotional responses, and cognitive responses, which is vital for lifelong learning and success.

Dylan's lively mind is at work as he finds multiple ways to examine the book through looking, touching, moving, and taking it apart. The *orientation* and *perspective* schemas are important in Dylan's investigation as he finds many ways to position his body to study the book more fully. Does he have an innate understanding that these different perspectives will help him see more? Will his brain build connections here that will help him learn to read later?

This moment is an example of how physical activity and schema explorations work together to grow children's brains. We have more questions we want to consider. In what ways does Dylan's ongoing physical activity enhance his learning in all areas? How does moving help him focus and grow his self-regulation? Does he use movement to contribute to his friendships with others? What more can we provide to challenge his developing skills? All this information will help us honor Dylan's active body, which is so central to the person he is in the world. Rather than thinking we should slow him down to sit still and listen to learn, we find his vital, joyful exuberance a delight to watch!

A Shiny Slide Story

With shared joy and purpose, the children zoomed down the gleaming silver slide they had intentionally placed on the hillside. Over and over, they followed one another up and down, sliding on their bellies and backs—inspiring each other to scoot, roll, and twist to move themselves along. Someone decided to add the challenge of holding a bucket on the way down, and soon everyone was trying that too. A large piece of fabric appeared, and the game changed again. The children devised the difficult task of pulling each other up and down the slide. Despite the struggle of this heavy work, the children had no doubt they could do it if they worked together.

Reflections and Questions

This story is a useful example of how schema explorations and active play work together to build children's brains and bodies. The children were lured by the thrill of the *trajectory* schema and the pure joy of moving their bodies as they went speeding down the hill. Their physical efforts engaged their proprioceptive systems. With their bodies fully stretched out, the children's bellies, backs, arms, and legs received input as they went skidding and bumping down the slope. They got big proprioceptive input from the strength it took to push and pull each other up and down too. The children's vestibular systems were also employed as they balanced and maneuvered their prone bodies to stay on the slide while avoiding the other children as they flew down together. All this proprioceptive and vestibular feedback strengthens existing and burgeoning connections in the brain.

What else is going on during this extraordinary experience? We try to imagine what the children may see, hear, and feel as they are surrounded by the reflective, bumpy surface of the very long slide. What might be the impact on the children's brain development as they are *enveloped* in the abundance of this sensorimotor world? Are the *orientation* and *perspective* schemas at play here as the children see and experience the world flying by on their way down the shiny surface?

Can you also see the children's powerful, flexible brains at work? The slide itself is an ingenious invention, and still the children added more complexity to the task by carrying the buckets and using the fabric for pulling each other. The children's natural ability to cooperate is also central in this story. Using very limited verbal language, they recognized and understood each other's schema play to grow this experience together. We marvel at the children's openness to be inspired by each other to try new ideas. The children's desire to help each other meet the challenges they set for themselves gives us hope that they will create a kinder world.

Jack's Bunk Bed

There was a quiet buzz as children were busily playing around the classroom. Suddenly we heard a soft giggle. "Where is it coming from?" everyone wondered. "Boo!" yelled a voice. To our grand surprise, it was Jack, who was hiding in the shoe rack! How did he squeeze his body into that tiny space? What inspired him to do that? The other children noticed Jack too, and we all laughed together as he pretended to take a nap on his "bunk bed."

Reflection and Questions

We take great pride in creating environments that are welcoming, beautiful, and homelike. Each school year, we work closely with our teaching teams to think about what new materials we might offer the children. Children consistently astonish us with the way they use items in unexpected ways. Although the shoe rack is not meant for children to use as a prop in their play, we were delighted to see Jack find such a creative way to *enclose* his body. Squeezing his body into that small space was not an easy task. Did he study the size of the shelf to determine whether his body would fit? Reflecting on the photo of Jack, we notice that he even used a pillow as part of his bed. Before learning about schema theory, we would have found this behavior annoying and an unsafe use of the furniture. Now we understand that children continually seek experiences where they can learn about moving and negotiating their bodies in the world. Jack's bunk bed and the other *enclosures* children construct are perfect avenues for them to receive the input their bodies and brains need. Designing and building an *enclosure* involves using the *connecting* schema. Fitting into a tight space calls on the *orientation* and *perspective* schemas, which require spatial reasoning and physical agility. The nests and tents children build offer them the cozy, calm feelings they relish from proprioceptive input through *enclosing*. Noticing the children's interest in these schemas, we make sure we have materials for building enclosures, such as fabric, big blocks, and big pillows, and ways to create hiding places.

Your Turn

Study these photos showing the many enclosures children have built in our rooms and think about the following questions:

- What skills and competencies do you think the children used to construct them?
- What do you think the children see and experience as they play in these places?
- What materials and spaces do you offer for your group to build enclosures? Observe how they use their minds and bodies in this play.

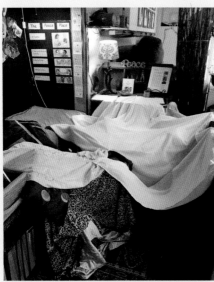

Schemas Invite Social Connections and Collaboration

Many of the children in our programs have vibrant personalities and exciting ideas they are eager to pursue. We find ourselves spending much of our time intervening with their conflicts to help them negotiate their big ideas. Recently we wanted to think more about the role we could play to support children's collaborative relationships, so we launched an informal teacher research project. Believing children to be competent, we used this question to observe and document their social interactions: What skills and strengths do the children already have for negotiating conflict and developing relationships?

Over time and with regular reflection, we learned a lot about children's abilities for social connections and collaboration. We documented multiple examples of children showing the following behaviors in their daily interactions:

- being welcoming and friendly
- delighting in being with others
- choosing to play together
- using nonverbal communication (body language, facial expressions, and tone of voice) to learn about others' ideas
- observing and recognizing the details of each other's actions and activities to share and grow experiences
- understanding and using humor to build connections with others
- noticing others' perspectives and negotiating different points of view
- being willing to engage in conflicts and work to resolve them
- eagerly helping each other and trying to make a useful contribution to the community

Of course we also saw conflict, but because we were specifically looking for competencies, we realized that children get along way more often than we think. When we stopped focusing solely on conflict, we were able to see its true frequency.

Reflecting on the many skills and competencies we documented, we uncovered that children recognize and are drawn to schema play in others. Schemas enable children to connect through shared ideas and actions. They can see the details of each other's play and can easily join in the play. Sharing schema play is delightful for the children because they can make a connection to someone and join in to offer more ways to extend the idea. They often engage in schema play using limited verbal language. They readily identify with the repeated actions they see their friends engaged in and can seamlessly participate and make significant and recognized contributions. Because verbal language is not essential for this cooperation, the youngest of children can use schema explorations to make connections and play well together.

Understanding that shared schemas are such a big part of children's cooperative play helps us see the role we can practice to support children's relationships. Rather than focusing on their conflicts, we can help children see each other's shared schema ideas and actions. As we describe the schemas they are engaged with, we know they will be able to recognize, understand, and use this information to further their play together.

As you read the following stories, notice the schema explorations that the children use to make connections, share ideas, and expand their play. You can also revisit the stories in chapter 2 to find more examples.

Where's Evan!

Gales of laughter filled the room as Evan, Kahaan, and Phoebe invented a game. Evan hid himself in the big box and immediately jumped out, to the delight of his friends. The children played the game this way over and over again, where Evan hid and then, with great anticipation, quickly burst out. But then Evan changed the game. Instead of jumping right out, he stayed covered up inside, being very, very quiet. "Where did he go?" Phoebe and Kahaan wondered. "Is he still in there?" "Where's Evan?" After several minutes and to great surprise, Evan popped out of the box again!

Reflections and Questions

Peekaboo is a simple game children begin to play when they are babies. Child development theory says that once children develop "person permanence" (the understanding that someone is still there even when you can't see them), they like practicing it over and over again. We believe there is more to this game. Underlying their interest in peekaboo is the pure joy children experience from the simple idea of "we see each other." In this game, Phoebe, Evan, and Kahaan remind us of the deep satisfaction we all feel through human connection.

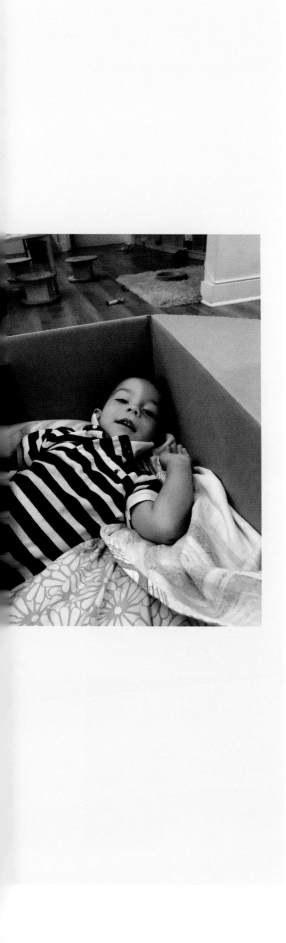

The children all know how to play peekaboo, and they seem to understand how to follow the simple rules to play this game together. But Evan added an intriguing idea when he changed the game. The children were excited as they anticipated Evan's actions, and Evan probably felt pretty powerful as his friends waited and called out for him. Because he stayed hidden for a long time, both Kahaan and Phoebe may have wondered for a moment if Evan was really still there. This thought added even more shared excitement to the game and real surprise as he popped out of the box.

This story illustrates how the children enjoy thinking about and practicing taking other points of view (*perspective*). Evan must have imagined what Phoebe and Kahaan were seeing and noticing about his actions. And they in turn wondered and even predicted what Evan would do next. Brain researchers call this understanding the "theory of the mind," the amazing notion that we have ideas, and other people may share our ideas or have different ones. This may sound simple to adults, but for young children, this is powerful new learning that is vital to their ongoing development.

As we study this game of peekaboo using our understandings of schema theory, we wonder if schemas are the mutual motivating force that brings the children together. Does the children's shared understanding of *enclosure* as Evan hides in the box help the game begin and enable rule making? Does the thrill of *transformation* as Evan is there one minute and then gone the next help the children see and share each other's *perspectives*? Our respect for these repeated patterns in the children's play heightens as we see the profound learning and the deep interpersonal connections that grow from this shared schema exploration.

The Roller Coaster

Xavier ran around the yard, eagerly looking for Jack. Finding him, he excitedly said, "Jack! You have to show Leelah how you made the roller coaster. I told her about it!" Jack responded with a cool voice and posture, "Oh, sure! I can show her." Jack told them what he would need, and Xavier and Leelah helped gather the items. Jack led them to a good spot to work and explained where each item should go. Together they lined up the upside-down trucks and put a big metal tub on top. "Leelah, you can go first. We'll take you for a ride." Leelah hopped in with a big smile on her face. As she held on tight to the sides of the bin, she was not sure what to expect. "Let's do a countdown," suggested Jack. "5, 4, 3, 2, 1, blast off!" The children rapidly pulled the tub across the wheels of the trucks, careful to stop when they got to the end of the roller coaster. Leelah squealed, "Woohoo! Let's do it again!"

Reflections and Questions

Teacher Nadia will never forget the day she first learned about the incredible roller coaster creation! She had just begun the classroom investigation about schemas with the children and families. Her coteacher Darby was excited to show her photos and a video of some of the schema work he captured in the yard. As they studied together, they were able to identify many schemas at the center of the children's play. The children were skillful in conceiving how to *transform* the materials into a roller coaster using the *connecting* and *rotation* schemas. *Transporting* and *trajectory* were central to how the children enabled the roller coaster to work. Nadia watched the video and was flabbergasted! She could not believe what she was seeing. It was beyond creative. It was genius! How did Jack come up with this idea? The children immediately knew how to join Jack in his construction. How did they come together so easily to work on such a complex idea? Had they ridden a roller coaster recently? Did the ideas come to them naturally as part of schema play? It took leadership, collaboration, idea sharing, problem solving, turn taking, and patience to make this creation come to life. What stood out to the teachers as they studied the documentation was the teamwork and peer mentorship. Their shared interest in Jack's idea brought this group of children together to explore this schema play. Jack shared his ideas and gracefully led a group of his classmates in putting the roller coaster together. The children listened to each other and invited their younger peers to join for a ride. The older children served as positive role models to guide their friends and provide support in both building and riding this amazing contraption.

The teachers wanted the whole community to know about the amazing work the children were doing together! Most importantly, Nadia wanted to see it for herself. Would the children build the roller coaster again? Would it be appropriate to ask them to re-create it? Perhaps the teachers could print photos and study the documentation with the children. The next day, the children were at it again. Nadia closely observed in awe as the children re-created this thrilling ride together.

Schemas Build Math Skills

We were excited when we discovered research that describes how children naturally explore math concepts through their play. The findings suggest that children's everyday play experiences form the foundation for later, more formal math skills and concepts. During observations of children's free play, researchers identified the following math concepts they explored (Clements and Sarama 2005):

- classifying: organizing materials by attribute
- exploring magnitude: describing and comparing the size of objects
- enumerating: saying number words, counting, instantly recognizing a number of objects, or reading or writing numbers
- investigating dynamics: putting things together, taking them apart, or exploring motions such as flipping
- studying pattern and shape: identifying or creating patterns or shapes, or exploring geometric properties
- exploring spatial relations: describing or drawing a location or direction

We immediately saw the connection between these findings and schema play, and we began to look for examples with the children in our classrooms. When the children are using the *positioning* and *ordering* schemas, they are working with classifying, exploring magnitude, and studying pattern and shape. Investigating dynamics grows from the *connecting* and *disconnecting* schemas and the *trajectory* schema. And the *orientation* and *perspective* schemas build understandings of spatial relations. Having new information and insight about the connection between math learning and schema play helps us be more intentional about planning experiences and offering materials that support children's development. We are eager to find more materials for launching cars and balls to encourage the *trajectory* schema in children's play. We search thrift stores for interesting containers with lids and dividers and for an abundance of gems, rocks, and other loose parts for children to sort and classify. It is gratifying to watch children naturally develop these important skills with the materials we intentionally offer. We can also call the children's attention to the math skills they are exploring as they engage with schemas, which helps them expand their actions and thinking. "When you match those buttons by their color and put them in a row next to each other, you are doing mathematics." Consider the following stories and those in chapter 2 to see if you can find the connections between math skills and schema play.

Serious Studies

Today twenty-month-old Harlan spent quite a long time discovering how to make small cars move down a plastic gutter. He used many different approaches, studying the results of each action he tried. With the ramp on his lap, he placed a car on it to see what would happen. It did not move to his satisfaction, so he changed the angle of his body to create more of an incline for the car to travel. This did not meet his expectations either, so he put the ramp on the ground to get some action that way. Again, he did not like what happened, so he put the gutter back in his lap. This time he created a steeper slope from his lap, and the car zoomed down. This worked just how he was hoping! With serious attention and delight, he raced the cars down the ramp over and over again. Next, using his understandings from these repeated explorations, he leaned the ramp off the stool at the perfect tilt to make the cars speed down.

Reflections and Questions

Do you see Harlan's brilliant and curious mind at work as he used the scientific method of trial and error to explore his theories and predictions? He systematically tried out each of his ideas, observing closely what occurred as a result of what he did, and then he tried something new until he got the results he was seeking. Harlan stuck with his ideas even though it was sometimes difficult for him to maneuver the ramp and his body together to meet his goal.

Does the thrill of exploring the *trajectory* schema sustain Harlan's efforts? His goal to get the car to move prompts him to practice many math concepts. As he is testing and retesting the angle needed to move the car, he is investigating dynamics and exploring motion: both are math concepts. The way Harlan instinctively maneuvered his body to get just the right slant reflects the *orientation* and *perspective* schemas where he used the math skills of spatial relations, location, and direction.

As Deb observed Harlan, she was tempted to step in to coach him on how he might be successful. As she watched, she saw that Harlan showed no frustration with this challenging work. He didn't need her help to figure this out. He just needed time to use his curiosity, skills, and abilities. In fact, intervening at this moment could hinder his initiative and send the message that the answers are beyond him. We believe the nature of Harlan's brain and the innate competencies and dispositions he uses propels his persistence through this challenge. Harlan's work here is remarkable. His joy, determination, and satisfaction in what he is learning shines through! Who knows, this experience could provide Harlan the foundational understandings of gravity and physics to use later on as a scientist or mathematician, inventing new ways to improve the world.

Camila the Mathematician

Camila's favorite thing to do in the class-room is explore the various open-ended materials offered in the art area. She cuts collage paper into tiny pieces and glues them carefully onto cardboard or yogurt lids. She finds the tiniest beads in the batch, gluing them onto paper to create intricate designs. She sees materials and has a clear intention of what to do with them. Her creations are one of a kind! Recently Camila has been designing clothing and accessories. She first draws her vision onto paper. Then she cuts pieces of fabric into squares and connects them with tape. She transforms her paper designs into various pieces of clothing, such as a dress or a scarf. Camila also enjoys drawing in unique ways. We watched her draw triangles and then continuously draw more triangles inside of each other, making them smaller and smaller until there was no more space for drawing.

Camila shows a love of ordering and positioning and organization. She makes very complex designs, sorting materials by color, shape, and size. Recently she took time to study a collection of Indian bangles, arranging them by color and positioning them on the stands. She also lined up a collection of corks in a specific design across the tray. We are amazed by the deep thought and focused details that Camila brings to her play. Her work is always stunningly beautiful!

Reflection and Questions

Parents and teachers worry about children learning academic skills and concepts such as math in preschool, and teachers often feel intimidated to "teach math" in preschool. By offering a variety of attractive open-ended materials, children investigate math concepts in a natural way through their play. An abundance of research suggests that by narrating what children are already doing (such as "Oh, Camila, I see how you've *classified* the bangles by color," or "Camila, I saw you *measure* the fabric to get just the right size for your dress"), we can increase children's math skills more naturally than using didactic instruction. The children show us their amazing flexible brains as they use these materials in so many different ways. This story, as well as many other stories in this book, shows us math is everywhere! How can we make the stories of children's skills and competencies visible so adults will relax and let children play?

Your Turn

As you study the photos of Camila's schema play, try to identify the math concepts she was exploring:

- classifying
- exploring magnitude
- investigating dynamics
- studying patterns and shapes

What materials are available in your environment that encourage children to explore math concepts? What more can you offer?

Try using materials to explore these math concepts for yourself. Engaging in this way may help you see that math does not have to be scary.

Invite families to explore the materials with you to help them experience how children learn about math every day.

Schemas Enhance Art Explorations

Research on the stages of art suggests that children's early work making marks through drawing and painting is random. The later stages of art where children use shapes to represent familiar objects are described as schematic drawing and painting. Children develop schemas for common objects, understanding that they can use squares to draw a house with walls and windows or circles to represent the heads and eyes of people. But when we focus our observations and study of children's work with paint and markers on how they use repeated actions to explore the materials, it doesn't look at all random. Even when children have not yet developed the schemas that inform their drawings of common objects, they are still using repeated patterns to enhance their art explorations. We believe children have an intrinsic understanding of the elements of art: color, shape, line, size, pattern, texture, space, form, unity, and balance. We have observed children doing the following when they are engaged in art experiences:

- moving their arms in a circular motion and making circle shapes (*rotation* and *circularity*)
- connecting lines and shapes together (*connecting*)
- placing lines and marks in particular places on a page (*positioning* and *ordering*)
- painting or drawing lines around the edge of a paper, totally filling in a shape or covering the entire paper with paint (*enclosing* and *enveloping*)
- mixing paints and other art materials to change them (*transforming*)
- using fast movements to get paint to splatter (*trajectory*)

Perhaps these kinds of schema explorations help children develop concepts for representing common objects later on. Or maybe, rather than representing objects, they are representing the schema explorations they regularly engage in using art materials. Study the stories and photos here to see if you can identify the schemas at work in children's art.

Paint Changes

Kahaan used the lustrous blue paint to create a circular shape on the brilliant white paper. Then he spent time filling in the circle with more blue paint (circularity and enclosing). Once the circle was completely covered in blue, he proceeded to layer other colors of paint on top. As he painted, he closely watched the impact of his actions, seeing the changes in the white paper and the way the colors mixed (transforming).

Reflections and Questions

Kahaan is just two years old, but it's hard to miss the seriousness of his work with schema theory in mind. How often have we disregarded a young child's painting, thinking they are just messing around? Can you see in Kahaan's innate desire to create a circle and then fill it up with paint, the many ways he is using the *transforming*, *enclosing*, and *circularity* schemas with this art exploration? In the past we have discouraged children from mixing paint. Now that we understand the significance and power of transformation on Kahaan's brain development, we are dedicated to protecting time for work like this. When we put ourselves in Kahaan's shoes, we understand the magic in this seemingly simple exploration. What new brain pathways does his work help him develop? Will he use these beginning experiences to build a repertoire of possibilities for more masterful art in the future? Our work is to see the importance of his explorations and help him do more.

Annette the Passionate Artist

Annette loves to draw and paint and takes advantage of these experiences whenever they are offered. Today she took up her interest in art with gusto! Chalk was available for drawing on the cement, but Annette saw a more interesting palette to explore. She gathered several different colors of chalk and, holding one piece in each hand, began to make lines and squiggles on the wooden planks set up for active play. She worked fervently to fill in spaces on one of the boards and then moved to the other one to add more marks. She literally enveloped herself in this work, covering the surface of both of the planks. Her head and face were hidden under her coat as she spread out on her belly, and then she used her entire body to stretch and move across the planks as she drew. She stayed focused, insistently drawing until the last possible minute.

Reflections and Questions

We are captivated by Annette's intensity for this big drawing. She brought her entire self to this work: body, mind, and emotions. How were schema explorations enhancing this art exploration? Were the *enclosing* and *enveloping* schemas enticing her to stretch her body to cover the space of the big planks? She also revisited the idea of *enclosing* by filling the space of the boards with chalk shapes. Study the photos to notice how *positioning* was on her mind and *orientation* and *perspective* were at play as she purposefully moved her body to find space to place the chalk marks. Was she employing the *transforming* schema as she changed the chalk marks using different pressure? Looking closely at Annette's experience underscores the notion that what she was doing was not random scribbling. Schema explorations deepen her understanding of the materials and grow her skills and ingenuity for creative expression. Her intensity reminds us of the passionate artist Jackson Pollock, who used big-body movement and intense emotion to splatter paint all over his canvases. We know that Annette will use her extraordinary talents and spirit to make a big impact on the world.

Love All Over the World

Carrick worked at the easel, using different colored paint sticks to make big marks all over the paper. Chris approached and asked to join. Carrick welcomed him, and together they used large-body movements to create bigger and bigger colorful lines, swirls, and scribbles. As their collaborative work continued, Carrick affirmed, "When we are done, it will be like love all over the world!" Although they did not say it out loud, it was clear they wanted to stand close together and fill the whole paper. When they were done, they stopped and looked at each other, smiling from ear to ear. The children were so pleased with the work they had done together that they asked Nadia to hang it up so everyone could see it!

Reflections and Questions

Schemas are everywhere! These repeated patterns in children's play even show up in their artwork. Children have the natural urge to fill space and to explore circles (*enclosing*, *rotation*, and *circularity*) as we see in this story. Five-year-olds Carrick and Chris were excited about investigating the *enclosing* schema by covering the entire large paper with circular marks and designs (*circularity*). What was their goal? Was this work about the task of filling the space or a sweet desire for a shared connection? Or perhaps both? This moment between the children had a deeper meaning for them. Earlier in the week, they had a conflict that was upsetting for both of them, and their hurt feelings lingered all week. Was their shared drawing using schemas helpful in soothing their feelings? Did Carrick's statement, "When we are done, it will be like love all over the world!" reflect a deep desire to resolve their conflict? In this story the value of shared schema explorations seems to go beyond simple actions to affect children in profound ways. Understanding that schema explorations support children in these meaningful ways compels us to offer materials that support their big interests and passions. Witnessing these powerful moments enhances our work and life!

Your Turn

Study the photos here of children engaged in art, and identify the schema explorations you see them using. Notice their attention to the elements of art: color, shape, line, size, pattern, texture, space, form, unity, and balance. Where do you find beauty in the children's work?

Schemas Advance Scripts for Imaginative Play

Children use shared play scripts all the time in their dramatic play. The schema for taking care of babies includes holding and rocking a baby to sleep, feeding, dressing, and changing diapers. Children also share scripts around other conceptual schemas, like pretending to be puppies and kitties, driving a car, and cooking and eating. Children share these understandings from their own lived experiences, which support their cooperation and grow their symbolic play. Different from these conceptual schemas are the repeated actions in play that we have been focusing on in this book. These schemas are the actions at work *within* the children's play scripts. For example, to put a baby to sleep, you need to wrap her in a blanket (*enclosing* and *enveloping*). Driving a vehicle involves pushing the car or truck up and down and around the yard (*trajectory* and *transporting*). Cooking and eating requires setting the table so everyone has a plate and a cup (*positioning* and *ordering*). Putting on dress-up clothes requires fitting your body into the openings in the clothing, or covering yourself with a cloth or cape and trying out a new character or identity (*enclosing* and *perspective*). We have observed children moving back and forth between schema play scripts and repeated schema actions. For example, children using sensory materials can focus on filling the cups and containers over and over again (*enclosing*) and then suddenly begin a cooking drama. The *enclosing* schema sustains the children's interest in the materials, and the drama grows from their repeated actions. These repeated actions during play could be the foundation for developing, sustaining, and advancing imaginative play scripts. Study the following stories to hear more of our thinking about these ideas.

Bye, Bye!

Malcom earnestly gathered up several bags and purses and draped them over his neck. He walked purposefully to the door, turned around, and began to wave, cheerfully singing out, "Bye, bye. Bye, bye!" He noticed Annette watching him and quickly rounded up more purses, insistently pushing them into her hands. She immediately understood his invitation, layered herself with the bags, and followed him around the room. They stopped together at the door, waving and calling out, "Bye, bye. Bye, bye!"

Reflections and Questions

Malcom and Annette share an understanding of the *transporting* schema, as well as the conceptual schema of "bye, bye"—getting your stuff, going to the door, and saying goodbye. These understandings make it possible for these children, who are not yet two years old, to invent a simple drama and act it out together. Their actions may seem unsophisticated, but underneath their play lie many skills and competencies. The children use skillful nonverbal communication as they read each other's body language and facial expressions to play collaboratively. They recognize that they share the same perspective and gain great satisfaction from playing this game together. We marvel at their discovery of symbolic play and the power of their imaginations. They realize that through their pretend play they can practice the difficult emotional experience of separation. We take seriously the way schema explorations enable the children to share in creating and pretending. We know these beginning play scripts will eventually develop into complex dramatic play that will be a source of powerful and satisfying learning throughout their childhood.

The Gumball Machine

To create this amazing contraption, Kaia and Nicolai lined up balls at the top of the safety mats and observed with anticipation as the balls rolled off. Kaia discovered that if she stood at the edge of the mats, all the balls would fly onto her head. The children laughed hysterically and immediately reset the balls to play the game again. This construction game turned into a drama as more children joined in, taking turns being the workers who set up the machine and the customers at the gumball store.

Enthusiastic to continue this imaginative play outside, the children worked cooperatively to rebuild the gumball machine using crates, ramps, and balls. They were persistent; it took them a while to figure out how to get the balls to stay in a line. Kennedy suggested using a crate to block the balls from rolling off. "It worked!" When the gumball machine was ready, the drama continued.

"Sofia, you can be in charge of passing out the gumballs. I'm going to get customers!"

"Okay! My machine is going to make lots of flavors."

"I can take the money from people."

The children ran around the play yard chanting, "Gumballs, gumballs, who wants gumballs?" "Gumballs for sale, gumballs for sale. Who wants gumballs?" Customers soon arrived. Bea charged them one dollar per gumball, and the children paid with their invisible money. Sofia greeted the customers and served different flavored gumballs. The children remodeled the gumball machine many times, using a variety of materials as this imaginative play continued for many weeks.

Reflections and Questions

The children's work was complicated and sophisticated. They used the blocks, ramps, and various loose parts over many weeks to create and re-create extremely detailed structures and invent complex dramas to go with their ingenious inventions (*connecting*). It took hard work to listen to one another's ideas and to imagine together, as they questioned, predicted, solved problems, and made decisions to grow these magnificent dramas. The children's shared schema explorations and attraction to open-ended materials advanced these unique, imaginative games. We wonder, were connections in their brains becoming stronger as they saw more possibilities for revisiting and reinventing the games?

These children are five years old, heading off to kindergarten next year. In this play, they are developing all the skills typically understood to mean *school readiness*—math concepts, enhanced vocabulary, fine- and gross-motor control, and social-emotional development. Yet this approach to play counters and goes beyond a limited "school readiness" agenda. The children are immersed in a shared passion for pretend play, initiative, and innovation. They experience their own competence and the power of their successful partnerships. We are dedicated to offering children opportunities for rich ongoing experiences that deepen their connections and learning.

Your Turn

Study the photos and the children's actions and conversations to build the gumball machines. Identify the schemas the children used and how the schemas contributed to the children's elaborate dramas:

- lining up the balls (*positioning*)
- putting the crates and ramps together (*connecting*)
- rolling balls off the mats and ramps (*trajectory*)
- seeing and sharing different points of view through constructions and drama (*orientation* and *perspective*)

Schemas Further Long-Term Investigations

We have found Piaget's description of a schema as "a thread of thought" to be extremely accurate. When observing children involved in play, you can see this thread as children repeat the same schema over and over while moving from object to object. Some of the research indicates that individual children often repeat the same schema during many different experiences. We also see children using many different schemas in one area or with a collection of materials. In fact, in studying long-term curriculum projects in many early childhood classrooms, schema play is often the underlying thread that motivates children's attention to revisit and deepen their learning about the project theme. Teachers often ask, "How do we motivate children's interest in a long-term project?" When we realize the appeal of schema explorations, we can plan and provide experiences and materials related to schemas that will hook children's attention to the project themes.

We started this book with a story about a chalk experience that resulted in a transformative teaching moment. We recognized the power and value of the *transforming* schema and let go of our adult agenda for children's use of materials. This first story in this section is a testimony to the power of schema investigations to promote long-term investigations, as Nadia's group continues to deepen their learning with multiple schema explorations of chalk throughout the year. The remaining stories similarly show the simple and complex ways children use these "threads of thought" to stay engaged over time, assuring deeper learning.

The Magic of Chalk

This morning, a group of children gathered on the outdoor stage with buckets, bowls, chalk, and Legos in hand. They grated pieces of chalk into containers, transforming the chalk from a solid to a powder. Once that job was done, they slowly added water, which transformed the powder into a thick liquid form. Usually, the creations are left in the buckets overnight, causing the mixture to turn into a hard, solid form. But today was different. The children used their hands to dig out the thick liquid from the containers. They rolled it in their hands, forming balls. Small balls, medium balls, big balls. When they were done, they put these "goo balls" on our saving shelf. After rest time, a group of children excitedly asked if they could go outside to look at their goo balls to see if they were still there. To the children's surprise, the balls no longer felt like goo. They were hardening. One of the children proposed, "Let's leave them there all night and see what happens!" The children and teachers liked this idea, and we left them there. Some children were worried that the younger children would take them, so we wrote a note that said, "SAVE SPOT!! NO TAKING!!!!!" The next morning, Nadia wondered if the children would remember to check on their chalk balls. Should she remind them or wait and see what the children would do? As children began arriving, they asked Nadia, "Can we go outside to check on our goo balls?" "I wonder if they are still there?" "Do you think they melted?" We went outside to investigate. To the children's relief, their goo balls were still there, and they were as hard as rocks!

Reflections and Questions

Chalk has become an important staple at our school. Children go home every day covered in chalk dust from head to toe. Take a peek into our yard and you will see every single bucket filled with chalk remnants, buckets of chalk experiments saved on doorsteps, and children deeply engaged in smashing chalk with shovels or other tools. The children also enjoy grating chalk with Lego pieces because it makes a squeaking sound like nails on a chalkboard. Teachers cringe when hearing this sound. It is absolutely one of our least favorite tools the children use. Yet chalk is an ongoing exploration for the children, year after year. It is also consistently a topic of discussion at our teacher meetings. As adults, we continually find it hard to support the children's fascination with transforming chalk. Recently Nadia asked a fellow teacher what her thoughts were about the children's use of chalk. She responded, "All I see them do is sit there with a Lego, grating the chalk, over and over again, day after day. *What* are they learning?" Her response reminded Nadia of herself not so long ago, when she could not see the value of this repetitive play either. She too was flustered by the wasteful use of the chalk. Her group went through boxes and boxes. As teachers passed out chalk to the children, all Nadia saw were dollar signs. She wanted to set restrictions on the amount of chalk passed out.

Learning about schema theory and practicing the art of reflective teaching, Nadia's perspective changed. This was not an overnight change, but one that took time observing, thinking, and understanding. Using this different lens, she could see why the children loved chalk so much. She saw the magic of chalk! In collaboration with her director, she facilitated discussions about the children's chalk work. They asked teachers to think about what the children may be experiencing when they explore the properties of chalk. This was often a controversial discussion among the teachers. Teachers shared their feelings of why they did or did not support the chalk work. Some feared that this work was encouraging children to destroy property and introducing them to graffiti. Many teachers wanted to set clear and strict guidelines on how chalk could be used. Nadia could relate to their feelings and wanted to help the teachers see the chalk work through a different lens. She invited them to take a closer look at the children's work and think about the children's perspective. What might the children be experiencing and learning through this type of play? Did they notice any schemas?

Using this new lens to observe the children's play, teachers have become more and more excited by the children's ongoing and complex use of chalk. They are amazed by how the children get to know the properties of chalk. They see children as scientists experimenting with *transforming* solids into powders—and then *transforming* the powder back into solid balls of chalk. The children's exploration of chalk and the teachers' own curiosity helped form a wonderful collaboration of reflective teaching. The children and the teachers have become a community of learners!

A Mysterious Hole

For the past several weeks, our eighteen-month- to two-year-old children have shared a fascination with a deep, dark hole they discovered in the wooden spool we added to the play yard. We have been amazed, amused, and curious as they continually find different objects to put into the hole and then eagerly look to see where the things went. Noticing this never-ending quest to fill the hole, we have been moving the spool to different places in the yard and positioning different materials nearby for the children to discover. They take up these invitations to fill the hole wherever they find the spool. The pink flowers quickly disappeared down the hole, and the sand offers a never-ending source to fill the hole. We supplied a basket of balls and leaned a ramp off the side of the spool to see if the children would push the balls down the ramp or fill the hole. They immediately put the balls in the hole. Enclosing the balls and looking to see where they went was definitely the main task the children were interested in pursuing.

After several weeks of filling the hole with random objects, the children invented a new game involving the older preschoolers, who visit them daily at the fence. One of the older girls offered Phoebe her shoe, and Phoebe immediately went and put it in the hole. The big girls laughed and teasingly begged to have the shoe back. Then another girl offered her headband, and it went straight into the hole too! This new game continued over several weeks. When we cleaned the yard, we were surprised to find many different items in the bottom of the spool, items we know came from the big girls. Our young ones didn't want to give anything back. Did they believe they were tricking the older girls? We are thinking about what we could offer as the next provocation in this investigation. Perhaps we could suggest that the preschool girls write a note asking about their missing items, to see what the toddlers would do in response.

Reflections and Questions

We are charmed as we reflect on the fascination the children have with this dark hole. This exploration is the *enclosure* schema, which on the surface seems like a simple cause-and-effect investigation. And yet this intrinsic desire the children have to fill an open space suggests so much more to consider about their learning. Here are some deeper questions we have been contemplating about the meaning of these *enclosing* explorations.

- Are they filling the hole again and again, looking to see where the objects go, because they enjoy the mystery of discovering the results of their actions?

- Are they assessing how their actions on different objects have different effects?

- Are they exploring the idea of things you can see and things you cannot see?

- Are they realizing that things usually show up again and speculating about where something that has disappeared will be?

- Are they grappling with uncertainty about what is unknowable and what is knowable?

The game the children invented to play with the older preschool girls involves a secret that all the children delight in. Taking and hiding the items is funny, and the younger children must feel powerful, thinking they are tricking the girls. They are trying on other perspectives as they imagine the big girls' thinking about the disappearance of their stuff.

The children revisited this work of using the hole for *enclosure* over several weeks. The thread of thought that we see in these repeated behaviors invites the children to deepen their thinking and expand this investigation from a simple cause-and-effect activity to a clever game involving collaboration and abstract thinking. Understanding the power of schema explorations allows us to notice and make plans to extend the children's learning week after week.

Again and Again and Again

It is Phoebe's first week in the toddler class, and she is safely tucked between Deb's legs as she stands working at the table, filling small cups with puff balls. Phoebe stays at this task for a long while, carefully fitting and refitting the balls—one, two, and three at a time—into the cup. She looks to Deb for several weeks to provide the protected envelopment of legs surrounding her as she works on more filling and refilling. Over the year, Phoebe's interest in filling spaces (enclosure and enveloping) shows up day after day in the choices she makes in her play. She is always drawn to the containers and cups ready to be filled with whatever objects are nearby. She also uses her body to explore her fascination with fitting things inside other things. Foremost is her thumb, which is always in her mouth. She steps on stones and wood rounds, balancing as she works to completely cover them with her feet. She also intentionally maneuvers her body to sit or lie on carpet squares and pillows. And she is the first to climb inside the baskets, boxes, and tents that are situated around the room.

Reflections and Questions

Phoebe is showing us the "thread of thought" from schema theory: a child using one schema over and over again. In Phoebe's case it is *enclosing* and *enveloping*. Her actions are intentional and persistent, and we wonder what motivates her. Does she seek to feel secure by being surrounded by her teacher's legs and feeling her thumb in her mouth? She's young and new to the group, so it makes sense she would look for ways to connect and develop trust. She instinctively understands that input from Deb's legs and her thumb affects her proprioceptive system, sending calming messages to her brain. Perhaps the security she feels from these comforting actions propels her to *enclose* and *envelop* objects too. Does she experience a sense of mastery and confidence when making things fit just the right way? Phoebe's recurrent and passionate interest in this schema exploration builds her confidence and skills for initiating and sustaining her learning. We characterize her repeated play patterns as an in-depth investigation, or learning project, that she naturally pursues. We believe our role is to notice her efforts, study what unfolds, and find ways to provision more materials for her to use to *enclose* and *envelop*. When we make her simple yet deeply important work visible to ourselves, to Phoebe, to her family and our coworkers, we are intellectually and emotionally engaged with each other. We can think of no better way to live our daily lives and create a better world.

Your Turn

Choose one child in your group to observe over a week to see if you discover any repeated actions or patterns in their play.

- Does the child use the same schema over and over again with different materials?
- Do they use many schema explorations with the same material?
- What seems to be the child's thread of thought?
- What can you offer to invite the child to continue and deepen their explorations?

CHAPTER 4

Environments and Materials to Invite Schema Explorations

The materials have their own inner life and their own story to tell. Yet they can be transformed only through their encounter with people. When we leave room in construction with materials, leave silence or pause or breathing room, that helps the materials themselves to express what they can express. —Elena Giacopini

We enjoy designing environments and offering collections of materials even more now that we understand the connection between brain development and the power of schema explorations. Children don't necessarily need special materials to explore schemas, because they use this focus in everything they do. Yet observing the remarkable ways children use materials motivates us to find more captivating ways to engage their amazing brains. One of our favorite quotes by Elena Giacopini (above), from the schools of Reggio Emilia, inspires us as we consider materials that will invite children to bring their lively minds to their explorations. What kinds of materials leave silence, pause, and breathing room? Certainly not most commercial toys, which can be used only one way and have limited sensory appeal; they restrict children's innate gifts for investigation and innovation. Materials that offer opportunities for discovery are open-ended loose parts, inviting children to move them around, take them apart, tinker, design, and build with them. The concept of loose parts is extremely popular in the field of early childhood education these days. Teachers eagerly scrutinize images of beautiful natural materials and unusual, open-ended, and recycled items for children's play and learning. Loose parts are promoted everywhere, including on social media sites like Pinterest and Instagram, in early childhood books and blogs, as well as by commercial companies that offer collections of loose parts for sale. We too are passionate about studying these beautiful images and resources for inspiration and, admittedly, to copy what we see. We can be easily enticed by all of the "cool stuff." But loose parts are valuable because of the substance they provide, not just the style. They shouldn't be treated like the next big fad. That's why we are also committed to continually expanding our understanding of why loose parts are so powerful for children's development.

Architect Simon Nicholson (1971, 30), who conceived the theory of loose parts, defines the importance of loose parts this way: "In any environment, both the degree of inventiveness and creativity, and the possibility of discovery, are directly proportional to the number and kind of variables in it." Nicholson's writing is a brilliant critique of the regimentation of education and the limited view of children's creative talents, particularly in relationship to the kinds of materials and environments offered for children's learning. He objected to the idea that only an elite few were considered to be worthy of creative endeavors. He predicted in his writing that the education system was on the verge of eliminating opportunities for most children to use their natural creativity and inventiveness because of the static environments and materials offered. With the push for outcomes, test scores and rating scales, and emphasis on controlling risk, a lot of what Nicholson foretold has come to pass. Yet the excitement about loose parts in many early education circles is a hopeful sign—especially if educators look beyond the fad to truly comprehend children's incredible capacity for using loose parts to learn through sensorimotor experiences and schema explorations. Nicholson's conviction to protect children's creativity and inventiveness is reinforced by the newest brain research and schema studies that we have been discussing in this book.

We share Nicholson's conviction and see our work as resistance to the regimented, commercial interests that pervade our profession. Children used loose parts long before there were toys or special invitations offered for their play. Watch a child anywhere there are objects to manipulate, and you will see their remarkable minds at work, with no planning or intervention by adults.

We believe our daily work of offering inspiring environments and materials to children is another way to promote democracy and social justice in the world. As you read the stories throughout this book, you can see that many of the materials we offer children are found objects, natural, recycled, homemade, and affordable. This makes them easily available and accessible. When materials are open-ended, they provide every child the opportunity to use them in their own way and to the best of their ability. Open-ended materials do not limit schema exploration the way close-ended materials can, thereby contributing to children's creative thinking skills.

Loose parts are also gender neutral because they can be defined and used in multiple ways and invite all children to explore them without being bound by gender roles. Materials like pieces of cloth or fabric instead of gender-defined clothing allow children to try out many roles. Expanding the kinds of materials in the drama center beyond kitchen props or baby care to include different kinds of containers and gems and fabric encourages expanded play possibilities. The block area can include a variety of treasures, such as shells, artificial plants and flowers, and carpet squares, to enhance creative construction. Provisioning our classrooms with loose parts with brain development and schema theory in mind helps us create equitable spaces where each child can be themselves and grow to their fullest potential.

Schema explorations occur in the many different areas of our classrooms, and with a variety of materials, both planned and unplanned, throughout the day. In this chapter we first introduce some principles that guide us in arranging the environment to meet up with children's minds. Then we offer categories of the kinds of play we see in our work with children and provide images and descriptions of the environment and materials we create to engage their lively minds.

Setting the Stage for Lively Minds

Setting up an environment, both the physical space and the collection and arrangement of materials, has a huge impact on how children play. To deepen our thinking and planning, we ask ourselves these questions as we observe children at play:

- What are children attracted to?
- What details do we see in their play that show us what they find engaging?
- Where and what materials do children play with for long periods of time and revisit again and again?
- How do the collections and arrangements of materials impact children's play?
- What play spaces and materials encourage cooperative play?

As we have gained more insight, we have identified some principles to guide our work:

Arrange equipment for children to move. Children's natural desire to move (*transport*) objects is a worthwhile schema on its own. Yet often when materials are dispersed all over the place, the children's focused use of materials is disrupted. Arranging tables and other equipment in a *circle* shape to create an *enclosure* will attract children to the play space. The children can *transport* materials from place to place inside or around the *enclosure*, staying focused on *positioning*, *ordering*, and other schema explorations. Revisiting materials and ideas in the same area, over time, encourages children's deeper discoveries. The children also find each other and can share actions and ideas more easily. Study the photos here and consider how children might respond.

Make the space and materials visible. Remembering that schemas are innate inclinations through which children see the world will help you consider the smallest details of their points of view and plan the environment for their attention and pleasure. *Positioning* a rug, a table, and even the top of a low shelf to suggest *enclosures* will beckon children to enter and stay to play. Your attention to *order* and *positioning* as you organize space and materials will speak loudly to children's attention to those schemas. Using open, flat, and mostly *circular* baskets, frames, trays, and mats also creates *enclosures* to highlight materials so children can clearly see and are drawn to what is offered. Study the photos here to expand your thinking.

Environments and Materials   113

Consider materials that appeal to children's super sensory abilities. We want to honor children's enormous capacity for taking in and organizing sensory information. Beyond the typical experiences of finger paint and mud play, we strive to surround children with magic, wonder, light, color, reflection, texture, and beauty at every turn. Study the photos here and consider the possibilities for engaging children's senses. What might they see, hear, taste, smell, touch, and move? What new ideas can you think of that would provoke wonder and magic?

Revisit schema explorations through differences in size and scale of materials. You can help children revisit and deepen schema explorations by paying attention to the size and scale of the materials you offer. Study the photos here and notice the children

- alternating between using small and large containers for *enclosing*;

- revisiting *rotation and circularity* with small manipulatives and larger equipment for active body exploration with hoops; and

- *transporting* materials with scoops and containers.

How do you think revisiting schema explorations in these ways affects children's learning? What other ideas do you have for giving children more ways to revisit schema play?

Categories of Experience

Rather than planning our environments around typical learning centers, we prefer to think about spreading different kinds of play and discovery all over the environment. Children do not confine their play to one theme, so we want to meet up with their lively minds to expand our thinking about what is possible. The following describes the kinds of experiences we plan for our environments and the collections of materials we offer. We hope you will be inspired by the photos here but challenge you to look beyond the beauty and aesthetics or the messiness and hassles. Instead, think about the marvelous children that will take up these invitations. What sensory delights are available to entice the children's open, flexible brains? What can they see, hear, smell, touch, or taste? How might the children move, change, design, invent, construct, and tinker with the materials? Try to identify all the possible schema explorations children will enjoy.

Sensory Experiences

Sensory tables and trays, sand, water, playdough, clay, paint, and other items, offered in abundance, combined with cups, spoons, containers, colanders, and additional items to move and manipulate the sensory substances, are foundational materials for sensorimotor and schema play. Planning for these typical early childhood materials with brain development and schemas in mind enhances the possibilities for children's long investigations and rich learning. Study the examples and reflections we offer, and think about the opportunities for your own environment.

This homemade water-play table with an invitation to wash baby dolls has many different possibilities for engaged play. The aesthetic beauty of the table's glistening tiles and soothing colors calls to the children's heightened sensory awareness. The galvanized tubs were placed intentionally to encourage *transporting* water from one tub to another. The different sizes and kinds of containers with a variety of lids and spouts invite *enclosing* and *transporting*. The sponges and soap, and the water itself, offer endless ways for *transforming* as the sponges fill with water and can be squeezed dry, the soap turns to frothy suds, and the water changes its form with each new container or the splash of a hand. Along with all the schema possibilities, the baby-washing props encourage pretend play.

How might this invitation of hundreds of buttons beckon children to the *trajectory* and *scattering* schemas? Can you imagine the sounds and other sensory possibilities here? How would you respond if the chidden used the materials in these ways? What other kinds of explorations are possible?

With great enjoyment and creativity, we work to provide unusual invitations for schema explorations. This magical invitation of ice was a huge success. The ice form was created with a container used for freezing water into the shape of a bottle cooler. The gems, animals, and real flowers were frozen inside the walls. The opening in the ice bids the children to use tongs to *transport* the ice cubes and fill the hole in the middle of the form (*enclose*). The children used salt and droppers of watercolor to melt the ice (*transform*). They were mesmerized by the changes of color and cracks that appeared in the frozen form. The ultimate thrill for the children was to unearth the treasures inside the ice. Melting wasn't fast enough, so they found tools from the playdough basket for hammering and pounding. With huge force, the children smashed the ice to smithereens, elated as ice pieces flew and water splashed off the table (*trajectory*).

Watching the grass grow over several weeks has been a thought-provoking experience of *transformation*. The children helped plant and water the tiny seeds and checked daily for new changes. The texture and smell of the grass entices the children's senses, and the opportunity to *transform* the grass again by cutting (*disconnecting*) adds to their deep engagement. What science knowledge will the children explore with this invitation?

How many different ways might the children use these invitations of materials? What schema possibilities can you identify in these invitations? Do you notice *connecting* and *disconnecting*? Can you describe the sensory delights that await the children?

Playdough is a supple material that can be manipulated and *transformed* by children. When offered with a variety of props and tools, the possibilities for many different schema explorations increase. Gems, buttons, and natural materials such as shells, stones, flowers, and herbs call on children's natural eye for design though the *ordering, positioning,* and *connecting* schemas. Sushi mats, craft sticks, candles, and small blocks can be used for creating *enclosures.* And unusual cups and dishes can be filled (*enclosing*) and stacked (*connecting*). Often the children will spend a long time covering the entire surface of the playdough with loose parts (*enveloping*). What elements of art and math concepts can you name here?

The flubber, or gak (made with glue, water, and starch), is a fascinating material for exploring *transformation* because it so easily moves, changes, and responds to the children's touch. The round white trays holding the bright-blue flubber and the tall round stool with the silky substance dripping from the holes call on the children's innate attraction to *rotation* and *circularity*. What else do you notice about the props and tools pictured and how children might use them?

How might the buckets hanging near water and sand invite children to explore *orientation* and *perspective,* or *trajectory*? What else is possible here?

Your Turn

Consider the materials and equipment you have available for sensory play. How can you create an invitation for your group of children that sparks their lively sensory abilities and provokes schema play? What combinations of materials can you collect and arrange to invite many different kinds of sensory and schema explorations? Offer an invitation to your children and step back to observe. What new insight and astonishment does their play offer you?

Big-Body, Active-Play Experiences

Paying attention to schema play possibilities when choosing materials and equipment for active play heightens the connection between children's physical activity and brain development. Often these types of experiences are offered in the outdoor environment, yet it is just as important to offer children active play indoors. Children are consistently seeking proprioceptive and vestibular input by finding ways to *enclose* their entire bodies, *transport* big items or themselves from one place to another, or jump up high and far (*trajectory*). Here are some examples of materials offered to invite active body schema explorations, both inside the classroom and outdoors.

Big tires, sturdy pieces of burlap, wheelbarrows, and crates all offer open-ended ways for children to explore schemas. Children use their big muscles to roll (*rotation*) the heavy tire up the stairs. The burlap is a strong material that can be filled with sand to *transport* around the yard. It is also strong enough to *transport* a friend. Children have the desire to make things fly from one place to another (*trajectory*). Study the photo where the teacher used crates and gross-motor mats to create an invitation for children to feel powerful as they jumped as high as they could. What other materials might you offer children to use with their active bodies through schema play?

Children love to wrap themselves up (*envelope*), hide in small spaces, and create *enclosures* around objects as well as their bodies. Children can *envelope* their entire bodies and get the proprioceptive input their bodies need with big pieces of stretchy fabric. Children build *enclosures* around themselves when provided with a variety of large loose parts, such as cones, spools, crates, and galvanized tubs. Teachers can also set up areas for children to feel *enclosed*, such as in this cozy corner of the classroom.

Noticing the children's interest in things that spin and roll (*rotation* and *circularity*), Nadia set up an invitation to explore painting with rollers. The children dipped the rollers in water "paint," stretched their bodies to reach up, and used big arm movements to "clean the school." After noticing he could not reach from the ground, Chris climbed to the top of the structure to clean every spot of dirt (*transforming*). Cleaning from the top of the structure gave him a different *perspective* as he leaned over and stretched to roll the tool up and down (*rotation*). What other items would offer children the chance to spin, roll, or turn objects and their bodies?

Children can often be seen *positioning*, *ordering*, and *connecting* objects to create a pathway for their bodies to follow. We have seen the innovative ways children explore these schemas, such as lining up blocks in the construction area to walk across, positioning a rope on the floor to use as a bridge, and gathering up piles of dirt in a row to jump on and smash. In these photos children used various loose parts to design and follow a trail.

Your Turn

Study the following photos of children using their bodies to explore the materials available. What schemas do you notice are possible? Can you envision using these materials in your program?

Observe children to assess your indoor and outdoor environments for active play. What possibilities are available for big-body schema explorations? What might you add to encourage more of this kind of play?

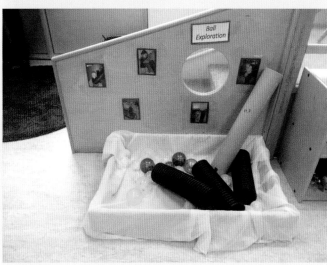

Building, Manipulatives, and Design Experiences

Most early childhood programs have blocks and other building materials that foster many different schema explorations. Rather than narrowing these experiences to the block area, we want to offer attractive, intriguing loose parts all over the room. These materials beckon children to add complexity to any kind of play. As you study the photos here, look for children's attention to beauty and *order* in their schema explorations. What math and science concepts are at work? When you see the brilliant way children use these materials, you will be inspired, like we are, to seek more resources to enrich their play.

Make sure you have many different kinds, sizes, and shapes of blocks in your environment. They are one of the best materials for all kinds of play and learning. Unfortunately, citing academic outcomes, many programs limit the blocks available for children's free exploration. Block play provides a wealth of experiences filled with pleasure and deep learning. These experiences can be even richer when there are a variety of beautiful and intriguing loose parts that children can add to their play. Study the photos here of children's play with these materials to identify the astounding ways they use problem solving, elements of design, and countless schema explorations. Can you find *enclosing, connecting, ordering, positioning, orientation,* and *trajectory*?

Study the photos here of the variety of intriguing materials and the astonishingly beautiful ways the children work with them. What sensory elements entice the children? What schema explorations can you identify?

Natural materials soothe and excite children's senses as they have shape, texture, color, and fragrance. Study the collections and offerings of natural materials here to delight in the variety and beauty and consider the schema play possibilities. Marvel at the gorgeous work the children have done with these materials.

Children's fascination with the *connecting* and *trajectory* schemas shows up when there are many suggestions for creating and following roadways. Study the photos here, showing invitations for children to *enclose*, *connect*, and zoom (*trajectory*).

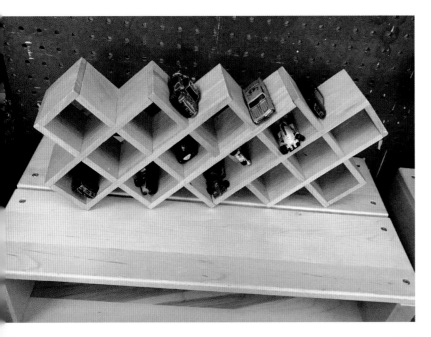

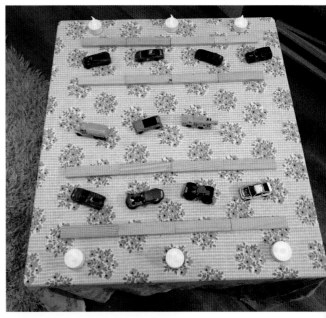

Exploring gravity, speed, motion, tilt, and angle are all physics concepts offered up during play with the loose parts pictured here. Children will be challenged by the problem solving and inventing necessary to use these materials. Can you identify how the children might explore various schemas (*rotation/circularity, enclosure, trajectory,* and *connection*)? As you watch children figure out how to play with these materials, your respect for their abilities will flourish!

Marbles are a different kind of magical ball. These colorful, shiny spheres speak to children's inclination to wonder. Children can use marbles to create designs (*connect* and *order*), swoop them around in a bin or sensory table to *scatter* them, and make them fly (*trajectory*). They can also be used with marble runs and tubes and ramps for *enclosing*, *connecting*, and *trajectory*. Are you a brave enough teacher to offer a bin full of marbles to your group of children? How might they respond?

Children dive in when they are offered collections of materials planned specifically for schema explorations. Examine the unique materials here and reflect on how children might use them. Again consider the sensory elements as well as the possibilities for problem solving and invention, and of course, identify all the schema explorations available.

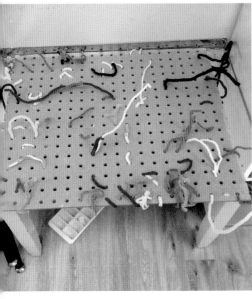

Academic Experiences

Although we do not believe in focusing our practice on a school readiness curriculum, we do believe that young children can learn academic skills and concepts through play. Children's play continually involves questioning, trial and error, problem solving, imagining, symbolic representation, and categorizing, which are the foundation of literacy, science, and math learning. And as children explore schemas, they are naturally pursuing science and mathematics. We want to draw on children's interest in schema explorations to invite them to learn the academic skills and concepts that will serve them well, now and in the future. We look to provide materials with the appeal of schema explorations that include identifying letters and numbers and exploring math and science concepts. Study the following materials to reflect on how they might introduce and grow academic skills and concepts.

Surrounding children with letters and a print-rich environment supports children's developing language and reading skills. Children can be exposed to letters while eagerly engaged in schema explorations with various items depicting the alphabet throughout the classroom.

Children can use these letters for sorting, categorizing, and lining them up (*ordering* and *connecting*) and in the process learn to identify the letters. Children will begin to use these materials in meaningful ways to find one another's names and to begin to form words. Take a close look at these photos. Identify the schema play available that invites children to explore literacy.

Just like schemas, math is everywhere! Children learn math through different play experiences. Materials that invite children to learn about numbers don't need to be restricted to the "math area." They can easily be added to many areas in the classroom. Can you identify in these photos how teachers have intentionally offered materials for schema play that children can use to explore math?

Helping children develop a love of science is easy and essential. Science involves inquiring, exploring, wondering, and making connections to the world around us, which children do all of the time. When allowed the space to observe, hypothesize, and problem solve, children can experience science in a hands-on way with natural materials. Study these photos where teachers have used children's attraction to schema play to set up invitations to explore concepts related to science and nature. What sensory and schema explorations will enlist the children's involvement?

The children have been transfixed by watching the caterpillars change to pupas and then to beautiful butterflies (*transforming*). The teacher has used their interest in these amazing creatures to offer puzzles and matching, sorting, and classifying games, all full of schema possibilities. Can you identify what they are?

Deb and her toddlers found an empty bird nest on their walk in the neighborhood one day. The children's intense curiosity encouraged her to offer materials for the children to explore schemas while also revisiting and learning about bird life, nests, and eggs. The children loved the aesthetic beauty of the materials and the schemas they were called to use.

These children were studying a local cave that has interesting formations of rocks inside. Their teacher offered them a schema experience that also helped them understand how the rock formations were created. She offered them watercolor, droppers, and paper upright on a stand. The children were absorbed as they layered streams of color over and over on the paper, watching the changes in shape, color, and thickness (*transforming*), simulating the process in nature.

Your Turn

Consider adding materials to your room that encourage schema explorations as well as expose children to academic skills and concepts. Observe how the children use the materials and the role you can play to help them learn more as they play.

Drama Experiences

When they've consolidated threads of thought that represent what they know, children possess scripts (schemas) for pretending to be cats or mommies or babies and so on. Children use a cat script to pretend to be a cat by crawling on their arms and legs, meowing, and eating out of a bowl. Or they use a mommy script to be a mommy going to work, cooking, and reading to their child. This symbolic play reflects a different kind of schema than we've been discussing in this book. Pretend play can spring up anytime and anywhere that children have access to open-ended materials. Yet we have observed there are some particular kinds of materials for schema play that easily encourage dramatic play. The children connect with and collaborate around shared schema play actions, which advance their shared drama scripts. Again, we don't limit these kinds of materials to the drama center and instead offer them throughout our environments.

Fabric lends itself to *enclosing* and *enveloping* while children create clothing and habitats for dramas. Children can also drape fabric to *transform* themselves, and they look through it to *transform* their view of the world.

Creating dramascapes for children to take care of babies or be babies themselves with materials that invite schema play will engage children over and over again. Baskets, beds, blankets, strollers, and even bottles invite the *enclosing*, *enveloping*, and *transporting* schemas.

Most children, even the younger ones, know the schema for birthday parties. Playing birthday involves cakes to cut, candles to blow out, and a song to sing. There are inviting commercial sets with playdough, and other items, like feathers and toothpicks for candles, that invite children's engagement. Schemas are a natural part of birthday play as the children create the cake, top it with the candles, and cut pieces of cake for each other *(transforming, connecting, disconnecting,* and *positioning).*

Dishes are a staple of dramatic play as children have experiences with them in their daily lives. Dishes also offer many opportunities for schema explorations as children can use them for *enclosing*, *positioning*, and *transporting*. Loose parts and sensory materials like sand, stones, and playdough lend themselves well as drama props for food and as schema props for *enclosing*, *transporting*, *positioning*, and *transforming*.

Your Turn

Observe your children engaged in dramatic play. What schema play do you notice they use as a part of their dramas? How could you extend their play with more props for schema explorations?

Identity and Antibias Experiences

Children are constantly sorting and classifying (*ordering*) the world around them. They identify different kinds of vehicles and animals, classify and sort toys (*order, position*) by their shape, size, and color.

They closely observe and classify people as well. Nadia came across a five-year-old child at the art table making a chart. He was an early writer and had created a list of a few of his friends. He then lined up little boxes and labeled them with the friends' different skin, hair, and eye colors (*connecting* and *ordering*). Deb has seen toddlers sort and line up (*connecting* and *ordering*) dolls by skin color and gender. Adults willingly work with children to identify and label the red truck and the blue car, or the cat and the dog. But when it comes to the characteristics of people, we are often uncomfortable because we have been taught that it is impolite or even racist to notice differences in people. Research on these topics suggests that from the time they are babies, children continually notice differences in people, and from the time they are two years old, they can develop prejudice. When adults show discomfort or remain quiet about differences in people, children begin to believe that something must be wrong, which can lead to negative self-identity, prejudice, and racism.

We continually bring a social justice lens to our work with children and use the goals outlined in Louise Derman-Sparks and Julie Olsen Edwards's *Anti-Bias Education for Young Children and Ourselves* in our teaching practices. We want to take advantage of children's natural interest in classifying, sorting, and *ordering* their world, including themselves and their friends, by providing materials for them to study their similarities and appreciate their differences in a comfortable, straightforward way. The experiences we offer are intentionally planned to work toward the first two of the four antibias goals, and as these experiences unfold, there are authentic opportunities to explore the other two goals (Derman-Sparks and Edwards 2010, 4):

- Goal 1—Identity: Each child will demonstrate self-awareness, confidence, family pride, and positive social identities.

- Goal 2—Diversity: Each child will express comfort and joy with human diversity; accurate language for human differences; and deep, caring human connections.

- Goal 3—Justice: Each child will increasingly recognize unfairness, have language to describe unfairness, and understand that unfairness hurts.

- Goal 4—Activism: Each child will demonstrate empowerment and the skills to act, with others or alone, against prejudice and/or discriminatory actions.

As you study the photos of children sorting and classifying (*ordering*) how they are alike and different, notice their interest and pleasure.

We offer a variety of opportunities for children to develop a positive self-identity through studying themselves and their physical features. We have conversations with the children about what they notice about themselves and about each other's similarities and differences (*ordering*) as they work side by side with mirrors and images of themselves. We regularly ask older preschoolers to draw and paint self-portraits, and we give younger children photos of themselves to draw on.

Homemade books, family portraits, sorting games, and drawing are experiences that encourage children to study others' families. Children are enamored with seeing their own family and sharing and comparing (*ordering*) the similarities and differences of each other's families.

This large box with a cover containing smaller wooden boxes with lids and latches is the perfect toddler material to invite *enclosing* and *enveloping*. The children are fascinated with opening and closing the box and working to attach the latch. Extra excitement comes with the photos, stickers, and other images that their families have used to decorate each child's individual box. The children love finding each other and their families inside and outside the box.

SKIN-COLOR MIXING

The children are engrossed in *transforming* paints to find just the right tones for their skin color. As they work side by side, they compare and contrast (*ordering*) each other's skin colors, coming to recognize that their differences are a normal part of being human.

Surrounding children with homemade books, matching games, and materials for play that reflect their identities calls on their natural interest in exploring how they are alike and how they are different (*ordering*). Natural conversations unfold as the children play with these ideas, growing a confident self-identify and appreciating one another's likenesses and differences.

Your Turn

What details do you see in your observations of children that show they are developing a positive self- and family identity and learning to appreciate one another's similarities and differences (*ordering* and *positioning*)? What new insights do your observations offer you? What materials can you offer to encourage these two antibias education goals?

CHAPTER 5

Making Schema Explorations and Learning Visible

Every school year, we look forward to discovering what new interests and strengths the children will bring to our classrooms. Together with the children and teaching team, we get excited about the topics of investigation we pursue. In the past we have learned about owls, jungle animals, architecture, spiders, and the human body. This year, Nadia was overjoyed to see the children using open-ended materials in new and innovative ways. Children used tubes, ramps, blocks, fabric, and gems to make elaborate creations. Little bricks, pine cones, rocks, wood, and shells became detailed *enclosures* for stuffed animals. Having learned about schema theory, she could recognize the repeated patterns and actions in their play. She shared her enthusiasm and knowledge about schema theory with her teaching team. They were as thrilled as she was and were open to learning about this theory with her. They found that having an understanding and awareness of the different schemas helped them understand the connections to children's developing brains and how important this play was for the children's learning. Schema theory helped them understand that children were not being disruptive or disrespectful with materials during this play. The children were instead responding to their natural inclinations, acting as scientists, testing out their ideas and theories.

Nadia and her team observed and documented the children's work to study during their team meetings. They brought photos of children's work they found fascinating or puzzling and reflected on the competencies they saw. They hypothesized which schemas the children might be investigating and provided the children with more materials and support for their inquiry. The team deepened their views of children's play, seeing the strength and brilliance in the work the children were doing. The teaching team was eager to discover what play would emerge next, what schemas they would notice.

The team decided that studying schema theory alongside the children would be a wonderful way to connect and share their excitement about the children's learning. They wanted the children to be able to see the brilliance in their work too!

They introduced the idea of schemas to the children at a morning meeting. Nadia showed the children photos with examples of some of the schema work the teachers had documented. She said, "Did you know that when you are making these types of creations, you are learning and your brains are growing? The work you are doing is so important that there is even a name for it: schema." She named the types of schemas she saw in the photos and showed the children a list of the other possible schemas. "We have been watching you work, and we are

really excited to learn about schema theory together with you! Your families are invited to learn with us too!" The children were excited to join us in this investigation, and it was the beginning of a meaningful collaboration.

Observation and Collaboration

By investigating schema theory together, the children brought their work to another level. After creating something, they would take a close look at their work and ask a teacher, "Is this schema?" Then the teachers and the children would look at the list of schemas together. "Oh yes, I see *enclosing*, *positioning*, and *sorting*," Nadia said while pointing to the details. Children began to look at their work with a peer and ask, "What kind of schema do you think this is? I think it's enclosure, just like the White House."

To support this inquiry, Nadia and her team dedicated an entire wall for ongoing documentation. Each child had a panel where examples of the schema work they were doing were posted. The children often helped teachers choose the photos and cut and tape them on their panels. Sitting down with a small group of children, looking at the photos, and reflecting on the different schemas showed that all the hard work they had been doing together was very special.

Family Involvement

Many children examined photos with peers and family members too. As parents or other family members came in the classroom, the children proudly showed them their schema board. They pointed to photos, explaining the details of their work, and identified the schemas. The teachers wrote newsletters and sent weekly email updates about this ongoing study of schema theory. They shared information about what schema theory is and invited the children's families to participate in this study. "What schemas are you seeing at home? What are you wondering about your child's play? We invite you to send us photos and descriptions of what you are noticing." Here are some of the responses we got from families:

From Robby's Mom

Robby teaches us something new every day. Recently he began to refer to many activities and games in our house as "schema." When we asked him about it, Robby said, "Schema is just what I do all the time. It is like, you build an airplane out of paper and then see how far it will fly. That is schema. It was a piece of paper, then an airplane."

Robby often asks us to take a photo of something he has constructed from Legos, magnetic tiles, or cardboard so we can send it to Nadia as an example of schema. When we ask him what makes it schema, he replies with a matter of fact, "Well, schema is something that I create from my mind, from my brain." "There are lots of schemas," he said, "like about ten hundred kinds. My favorite is construction schema."

From Jack's Dad

*After seeing the photos and reading about the roller-coaster creation, we were completely amazed, inspired, and proud. Every night we read a story to Jack, and two particular authors we have all come to enjoy are Chris Van Dusen (*If I Built a House *and* If I Built a Car*) and Andrea Beaty (*Iggy Peck, Architect *and* Rosie Revere, Engineer*). In their books, both authors have their main characters use their imagination and items around them to create amazing things. Through this learning, we now have a child who is encouraged to see beyond the intended purpose of an item and to create new and amazing creations limited by no boundaries or obstacles.*

As the families learned about schema theory, they observed more when they spent time in the classroom. The children would often invite their family member to collaborate in creating with open-ended materials. It was great to see those adults playing and thinking about schemas alongside the children.

The Role of the Teacher

Not only did the children take their work to another level through this investigation, so did the teachers! Nadia and her team were very proud of the work they did together as a teaching team. They have been on a journey of learning about reflective practice for many years now. Learning to take the time to pause and reflect on what is really happening helped them see the children's big ideas come alive. Reflective practice is no easy task. It takes a lot of work and commitment, and the ability to see yourself as a learner. Teachers must be open to examining their own reactions and to hearing the perspectives of others. In the beginning, it was a challenge to see the possibilities of how the children could use the materials in the yard, which is a shared space. Sometimes teachers stopped the children's play. Some worried about safety, while others worried about being respectful of the materials. They did not agree with children using so many materials or with the children using them in "inappropriate" ways. One teacher worried about equity. "I want to make sure other children have equal access to the trucks, or at least are offered a spot in the games. That game uses every truck on the playground!" Nadia wondered how she could help the teachers see the brilliance in the children. With the support of the school directors, Nadia used a professional development day to share observations and learning with her colleagues. She prepared a slideshow presentation to introduce schema theory. To inspire the teachers' thinking, she shared a video of a group of children building the roller coaster. Afterward she prepared a hands-on activity. Nadia asked teachers to get in small groups and find things in their pockets, purses, or bags to design a machine. The teachers showed great excitement as they collaborated with their teams and used their imaginations to make something out of ordinary materials. After their play, they reflected on their experience with these questions from the Thinking Lens (Carter and Curtis 2010):

- **Know yourself:** What captures my attention as the children engage, explore, and interact? What challenges and delights me as I watch and listen? How do my background and values influence my response to this situation and why? What adult perspectives (standards, health and safety, time, goals) are on my mind?

- **Find the details of the competent child:** What theoretical underpinnings are apparent in the children's ideas about how to build a roller coaster? How did their work reflect brain development facts?

- **Child's point of view:** How did your work to make a machine help you see the children's point of view? Why do you think the children were so engaged in this work together?

- **Reflect and take action:** How might seeing children's competence and the amazing capacity of their brains inform your work?

The directors and teachers were astounded at the work the children had done to create the roller coaster. The story showcased what children are capable of when teachers put their initial worry aside and observe the details and significance of the children's work. Teacher Mahroushka shared the following thoughts about the presentation:

"AMAZING CREATION! Wow! After seeing that video, I thought about the harm of a teacher showing them how to do it but also the lost experience if a teacher stopped it due to concerns of safety as opposed to just doing a safety check so all are comfortable.

"I may have honestly stopped it prior to all the work we've been doing on reflective practice. If I hadn't slowed down enough to see their concept, I may have become nervous. Definitely an exciting concept and something that continues to be a deep interest for the children as I just witnessed Kennedy and Miles building a roller coaster a few days ago. Miles told me that Jack built the first one."

Teacher Haruka also wrote a reflection about the roller coaster:

"My initial thought about this roller coaster was what a great innovation it is. The creation is genius, and the children can clearly think outside the box. It blew my mind how they used the trucks upside down. Personally, if I were a creator, I don't think I would have

thought of flipping the trucks. Furthermore, the children utilized the mobility of the flipped trucks as a rail. This idea to use the bucket as a car to roll over the flipped trucks left my jaw hanging. It was a shocking moment. I witnessed engineers, physicists, artists, and innovators right in front of my eyes. It was quite magical.

"If we weren't familiar with reflective practice, this play wouldn't have happened at all. I would have thought this play was dangerous and wouldn't have let children glide through the tracks, let alone sit in a bucket on top of flipped trucks. Because of Pacific Primary's philosophy, such as reflective practice, I felt confident watching after this play with close supervision. The beauty of reflective practice is that the ideas can grow up to their potential and the unthinkable creations can ultimately surprise people, like what Jack did to me."

Through this experience, Nadia identified the following ways to help teachers see the brilliance in the children's play:

- Highlight the children's schema play through photo documentation.
- Share stories of children's ideas and actions during every staff meeting.
- Study the children's play with all the teachers.
- Model while in shared spaces how to slow down, observe, and let children explore and be creative with materials.

Teachers became curious about schema theory. Many of them observed and studied children's play in their own classrooms, looking for recurring schema themes. What teachers had seen as challenging or bothersome play now looked like clever work that they wanted to support and extend. Together they began to understand children's schema play and the amazing connections happening in their brains.

Schema Superpowers

As they made the children's work and thinking visible to them, their peers, and their families, the teachers saw a change in the way the children saw themselves. The children showed great pride in their work. They became reflective thinkers, studying their own work and that of others. They identified schemas and asked for their work to be documented with a camera. They saw themselves as competent learners. They collaborated and communicated with their peers, teachers, and parents about the importance of the work they were doing. The adults in their lives were sharing in this meaningful work. Their ideas were being heard and validated. As one of the children said, they had become "schema superheroes." What would your schema superpower be?

"Building a diamond from anything."

"Being able to see any schema."

"Making pretend things real."

"Building really big houses with magnetic tiles."

"Transforming myself into an invisible person."

"Making one giant gumball machine."

We hope this story and this book inspire you and your children to become schema superheroes!

APPENDIX A

Meeting Up with Children's Lively Minds
A Tool for Observation and Reflections of Schema Play and Brain Development

OBSERVING CHILDREN'S PLAY

- What details do you see as children engage in play?

- Where in the environment are the children playing, and what materials are they using?

- Who and how many children are playing? What roles are each of them taking during the play?

- How long are the children staying engaged in the play? How has the play changed or evolved during the time you are observing?

- How are children using their bodies for active play?

- What schema explorations do you see the children pursuing? How do you see the children using their flexible brains to learn in many ways?

REFLECTIONS AS YOU OBSERVE THE PLAY

- Did you plan the play environment for the children? If so, are they playing how you hoped?

- Did the children initiate the play on their own? If so, what surprises, challenges, and delights you as you watch them play?

- Is there anything the children are doing that you feel concerned about and need to intervene (safety, social conflict, and so on)? Can you wait and watch for a few more minutes before you intervene?

- If you did not intervene, how did the children work things out for themselves?

- If you did intervene, what did you do and what was the result? How do you feel about the role you played?

- What delighted and inspired you about the play you saw? Why?

- What details did you observe during the play that show the children's competence? What details showed the children using their flexible brains to learn in many ways?

- Identify as many schema explorations that you noticed during the play. Was there one schema the children used more often, or did they cycle through many different schemas?

- What about the environment and materials supported and extended the children's play and schema explorations?

- How did you see children expand their play through connecting with each other around schema explorations?

- How did the children use active play in their schema explorations?

- What role did you take on to support or extend the play? How did the children respond? Is what happened what you hoped for? How did you use your understanding of schemas to inform the role you played during the play?

PLANNING FOR SCHEMA PLAY

- What new thinking do you have as a result of this observation?

- What are you excited to try next with the children after this observation?

- What changes in the environment would support and expand children's schema explorations?

- Identify new materials you can add to support specific schema explorations you observed.

- What new roles do you want to play during the children's play?

- How will you share what happened during this playtime with the children, families, and your coworkers?

APPENDIX B

Summary of Schema Explorations

When children are exploring schemas, they are growing brain connections as they build understandings of abstract ideas, patterns, and concepts. Once you start looking, you will see them everywhere in children's play. Observe for schemas to meet up with and plan for children's lively minds and amazing capacity for learning.

TRANSPORTING

With earnest intention, children regularly take up the work of moving objects from one place to another. Often, once they get the object to a destination, they do nothing with it. Using vehicles like trucks and wagons, large and small containers, bags and purses, cups and pitchers, children are absorbed with the pure joy and satisfaction of moving objects and themselves.

TRANSFORMING

Children engaged with the transforming schema almost always have a mesmerized look on their faces. They slow down to study the powerful changes they can produce when exploring paint, water, sand, clay, and building with open-ended materials.

TRAJECTORY

Children find endless ways to propel objects and themselves. They are exhilarated when running, swinging, pushing, pulling, and launching themselves through the air. They love to make balls fly, cars zoom, and blocks crash, and even babies delight in watching their bottles fall as they drop them to the ground from their high chairs.

ROTATION AND CIRCULARITY

Children delight in spinning till they are dizzy, rolling down hills, and joyously running and dancing around. They also have a strong interest in exploring wheels, balls, knobs, and anything else that can be rolled, turned, twirled, twisted, or spun. They enjoy seeing and creating curved lines and circles.

ENCLOSING AND ENVELOPING

Children seem to have a spiritual quest to fill a hole or build and climb into a cozy space. It is impossible to count the number of times children fill cups, bowls, and purses with nearby objects, or climb into boxes, cupboards, tents, or other small spaces.

CONNECTING AND DISCONNECTING

The essential strategies children use to try out ideas and consolidate understandings as they investigate the world is to study how materials can be linked and their relationship to one another. They do this by putting things together and taking them apart, connecting and disconnecting, scattering, and assembling and disassembling.

POSITIONING AND ORDERING

Young children are constantly noticing similarities and differences and sorting and classifying everything. They are doing this with people, other living creatures, as well as objects. You will observe children spending time carefully placing objects in lines, patterns, or sequences, and putting them in groups.

ORIENTATION AND PERSPECTIVE

Children continually seek to view the world from many perspectives. They place themselves in interesting positions by climbing up high, lying on the floor, seeing the world sideways, hiding under furniture, hanging upside down, and peering through translucent objects or at mirrors.

References

Atherton, Frances, and Cathy Nutbrown. 2016. "Schematic Pedagogy: Supporting One Child's Learning at Home and in a Group." *International Journal of Early Years Education* 24 (1): 63–79.

Athey, Chris. 2007. *Extending Thought in Young Children: A Parent-Teacher Partnership*. 2nd ed. Thousand Oaks, CA: Sage Publications.

Brommer, Gerald F. 2010. *Illustrated Elements of Art and Principles of Design*. Glenview, IL: Crystal Productions.

Carter, Margie, and Deb Curtis. 2010. *The Visionary Director: A Handbook for Dreaming, Organizing, and Improvising in Your Center*. 2nd ed. St. Paul, MN: Redleaf Press.

Clements, Douglas H., and Julie Sarama. 2005. "Math Play: How Young Children Approach Math." *Scholastic Early Childhood Today* (January/February):50–57.

Derman-Sparks, Louise, and Julie Olsen Edwards. 2010. *Anti-Bias Education for Young Children and Ourselves*. Washington, DC: NAEYC.

Gopnik, Alison. 2009. *The Philosophical Baby: What Children's Minds Tell Us about Truth, Love, and the Meaning of Life*. New York: Farrar, Straus and Giroux.

Hanscom, Angela J. 2016. *Balanced and Barefoot: How Unrestricted Outdoor Play Makes for Strong, Confident, and Capable Children*. Oakland, CA: New Harbinger Publications.

Lima, Manuel. 2017. *The Book of Circles: Visualizing Spheres of Knowledge*. New York: Princeton Architectural Press.

Nicholson, Simon. 1971. "How Not to Cheat Children: The Theory of Loose Parts." *Landscape Architecture* (October):30–34.

Piaget, Jean. 1952. *The Origins of Intelligence in Children*. Translated by Margaret Cook. New York: International Universities Press.

Index